Western Union Telegraph Company

The Proposed Union of the Telegraph and Postal Systems

Statement of the Western Union Telegraph Company

Western Union Telegraph Company

The Proposed Union of the Telegraph and Postal Systems
Statement of the Western Union Telegraph Company

ISBN/EAN: 9783337192532

Printed in Europe, USA, Canada, Australia, Japan

Cover: Foto ©Andreas Hilbeck / pixelio.de

More available books at **www.hansebooks.com**

THE

PROPOSED UNION

OF THE

TELEGRAPH AND POSTAL SYSTEMS.

STATEMENT

OF THE

WESTERN UNION TELEGRAPH COMPANY.

CAMBRIDGE:

WELCH, BIGELOW, AND COMPANY,

PRINTERS TO THE UNIVERSITY.

1869.

CONTENTS.

REVIEW OF MR. GARDINER G. HUBBARD'S LETTER TO THE POST-MASTER-GENERAL ON THE EUROPEAN AND AMERICAN SYSTEMS OF TELEGRAPH.

PROGRESS OF THE ELECTRIC TELEGRAPH IN AMERICA AND EUROPE.

REASONS WHY GOVERNMENT SHOULD NOT ENTER INTO COMPETITION WITH THE PEOPLE IN THE OPERATION OF THE TELEGRAPH.

REVIEW

OF

HON. E. B. WASHBURNE'S PAPER ON THE UNION OF THE TELEGRAPH AND POSTAL SYSTEMS.

IN the second session of the Fortieth Congress, 1868, a bill was introduced and a paper submitted by Hon. E. B. Washburne, of Illinois, relating to the "Union of the Telegraph and Postal Systems" in the United States, which has naturally attracted public attention, and especially of that large class of our citizens who are identified with the Telegraph interests of the country. The paper bears upon its face such evident marks of care, and the case is presented with so much earnestness and apparent sincerity, notwithstanding the frequency of its errors and the illusory character of its appeals to the practice and experience of foreign nations, that it cannot fail to produce upon the public mind an unjust impression that the usefulness of this great invention is injuriously restricted, and its operations unfaithfully managed, by the organizations having it in control.

To correct these erroneous impressions by calmly and respectfully criticising the statements thus presented, and proving the honesty and fidelity with which the Telegraph service is performed in this country, is the object of this paper.

A MERITED COMPLIMENT TO PROFESSOR MORSE.

In the acknowledgment made by Mr. Washburne, in the opening of his paper, that "the world is indebted to the genius of a citizen of the United States for the practical development of the electric telegraph as a means of communication," we heartily concur. That citizen is still a member of the Company to which his

1

great discovery gave birth, and on whose success he largely depends for support. To it he gives his ripened genius and matured wisdom, justly priding himself upon the success of his invention, and desiring for it the largest and widest use.

But Professor Morse needs more than the simple honor of making a great discovery and of placing it at the disposal of his fellow-men throughout the world, and when it is considered that the effect of the system proposed to be inaugurated by Mr. Washburne's bill would be the inevitable destruction of all existing telegraph investments, and possibly the impoverishment of the great inventor himself, the compliment seems a barren one indeed.

CONGRESSIONAL AID.

Congress, it is true, aided the introduction of the Telegraph by an appropriation of thirty thousand dollars for a public experiment and test of its capacity. But it may well be questioned whether this appropriation was not, after all, an injury rather than a benefit, both to the inventor and the people. It left no property to enrich its possessors, and no models to guide them in erecting new structures, while it was obtained by sacrifices which have cost the inventor infinite sorrow, and clouded a score of years with litigation. The time occupied by Congress in the consideration of the offer of the invention to government for one hundred thousand dollars (which was rejected) consumed nearly two years of the patent, and exposed the inventor to the endurance of a most annoying uncertainty.

Government, however, most effectually insured its successful extension, when, contrary to the practice of European powers, it declined to assume the control of the Telegraph, and referred its inventor, after the thorough investigation of the Postmaster-General, to the people as the proper recipients of his discovery. It was the healthy act of a government which recognized its duty to protect, instead of absorbing, the enterprises of its citizens. That duty is as clear to-day as it was then.

When government rejected the control and ownership of the Telegraph, although offered for so paltry a sum by the inventor, it was accepted by the people as a legitimate enterprise, and they have given to it all the **capital,** skill, and labor required for the fullest **development of its usefulness.**

Although **many** years elapsed after the introduction of the Telegraph in this country during which **it** maintained but **a feeble** existence through numerous weak and limited organizations, **that** rendered the business expensive and precarious, it now begins **to** crystallize into strength and harmony; and the projectors and promoters of the enterprise feel that they have a right to expect the fruit of their labors, in the proper and legitimate return which the humblest citizen receives for his work, and which government was, in part at least, organized to **secure.** We therefore pronounce the Washburne bill an **unwarranted and** unjust measure, **which,** while proposing **an** ostensible public good, essays to provide it **by** the destruction of vast private interests for which it proposes no **compensation.**

ERRONEOUS CHARGES AGAINST THE AMERICAN TELEGRAPH SYSTEM.

To the charges **made by** Mr. Washburne, in the prefatory **sentences** of his paper, against the management of the Telegraph **system** of the United States, little need be said. **They are** without the shadow of proof, and require no other answer than an explicit denial. Yet American telegraph companies may justly complain that a public man, while ostensibly performing a service **in** the interests of the people, should deem it necessary to traduce **a** vast interest **by the** use **of terms so** broad as **to** attract to **it,** even **without proof of their justice, unwarranted** disparagement and suspicion.

Mr. Washburne's **statement that "the telegraphic system has** made less progress **toward perfection, and has been practically** of less value **to** the masses of the people **in** our country, than **in any** other civilized **country** on the globe," is so sweepingly **erroneous** as to excite **our** profound astonishment, which is **increased by** the still broader assertion that, "while in nearly **every** country in Europe the telegraph has become a speedy, **certain, and** economical medium of communication, the inestimable benefits of **which** are **extended to** the inhabitants of **small towns** and communes as well as to the great centres of trade, in this country telegraphic communication has always been uncertain and expensive, and limited to chief towns and cities."

BRIEF STATEMENT OF FACTS.

In reply to the above we desire to present the following facts.

The population of Europe at the last authentic census was 288,001,365, nineteen twentieths of which belonged to the Caucasian race. It contains thirty-nine cities, each possessing more than one hundred thousand inhabitants, and the accumulated wealth of nearly two thousand years of civilization.

The United States has a population of only 31,148,047, and contains but ten cities of one hundred thousand inhabitants, while its utmost civilized history reaches back scarcely two and a half centuries, and the accumulated wealth of its civilization cannot average fifty years throughout its cultivated area.

The population of Europe being nearly ten times greater than that of the United States, as is also its accumulations of years of civilization, while, according to Mr. Washburne, its telegraph facilities vastly outstrip ours, it should, of course, possess far more than ten times the number of telegraph offices.

But, in truth, there is not even an approximation to this provision of telegraphic convenience based on population ; for while the United States alone possess 4,126 telegraph offices, all Europe contains but 6,450, of which 2,151, or more than one third of the whole number, belong to Great Britain, where the telegraph has heretofore been free from government control.

It is significant of American enterprise that continental Europe, with a population of 260,000,000, possesses but one hundred and seventy-three more telegraph offices than the United States, with her 31,000,000 of widely scattered people. While in the United States there is a telegraph office to every 7,549 of its inhabitants, in continental Europe there is only one to every 60,249!

The following table will serve to show the proportion of telegraph offices to population in the principal countries of Europe and of the United States, the number of miles of line, and amount of telegraph business of each.

TABLE A.

Statistics of the Telegraph in Europe and America for the year 1866,
from official reports.

Countries.	Number of Stations.	Miles of Line.	Miles of Wire.	Total Number of Messages Transmitted.	Population.*	Proportion of Offices to Population.
Austria	856	24,618	73,854	2,507,472	39,411,309	1 to 46,311
Belgium	356	2,187	6,146	1,128,005	4,530,228	1 to 12,416
Bavaria		2,115	4,945			
Denmark	89		2,515	308,150	1,684,004	1 to 18,921
France	1,209	20,628	68,687	2,842,554	38,302,625	1 to 31,681
Great Britain and Ireland	2,151	16,588	80,466	5,781,189	29,591,009	1 to 13,750
Italy	529	8,200	20,120	1,760,889	24,550,845	1 to 49,000
Norway	73			269,375	1,433,488	1 to 19,773
Prussia	538	18,386	55,149	1,964,003	17,739,913	1 to 32,955
Russia	308	12,013	22,214	838,653	68,224,832	1 to 221,508
Switzerland	252	1,858	3,715	668,916	2,534,240	1 to 10,000
Spain	142	8,871	17,743	533,376	16,302,625	1 to 100,000
United States	4,126	62,782	125,564	12,904,770	31,148,047	1 to 7,549
Dominion of Canada	382	6,747	8,935	573,219	3,976,224	1 to 10,400

In large sections of the United States the proportion is much greater. Thus, the Pacific States embrace an area of 600,000 square miles; Belgium, 11,000. The former provide an office to every 2,500 of their population; the latter, one to every 12,416. Thus, the Pacific States sustain five times as many offices in proportion to population as Belgium, to say nothing of the great disparity in the condition of service by the vast range of wild territory occupied by the one, and the fine roads and cultivated area of the other.

In view of the facts shown in the preceding table, how can it be said that in America the telegraph is less practically provided to the people than in any other civilized country on the globe?

THE COMPLAINT OF INDIFFERENCE TO PUBLIC CONVENIENCE WITHOUT FOUNDATION.

" Instead of an auxiliary to the postal system, controlled, like it, by the state, sought, like it, to be made useful to the great masses of the people without regard to the pecuniary profit to be secured, as in nearly every civilized country in the world, we see the system in this country in the hands of rival companies, anxious only for profit, extending their lines only to prominent places where such profits are to be secured, and too indifferent to the public convenience. In short, the popular verdict of the

* From the Annual Cyclopædia. New York: D. Appleton & Co. 1868.

people of this country, if it could be heard, would be that the telegraphic system, in view of what it is in other countries and might become in this, is practically a failure."

The above complaint is without the least foundation. In no country in the world is there so vast a system of lines under one control as in this; in no country is the business done so well or so cheaply; and nowhere else has there ever been so earnest an endeavor made to serve the people faithfully and satisfactorily.

A great majority of the towns in this country having even less than five hundred inhabitants are already supplied with offices, and they are rapidly increasing. During the past two and a half years more than one million of dollars have been spent by the Western Union Telegraph Company alone in the construction of new lines, and during the same period it has opened more than eight hundred new offices. This it is constantly doing, as much to satisfy existing public wants as for the promotion of its own future interest. Over one hundred offices have long been sustained at a loss, because needed to protect the lines built through comparatively desert regions to reach distant points of intercourse, and several hundred more are maintained which barely pay expenses. In fact, it is a standing rule of the company to open and maintain a telegraph office at all places in the United States reached by its lines, on a guaranty that the receipts shall be equal to the necessary expenses; and, by associating the duties of the telegraphic service with other productive labor, they are often rendered extremely light. It also offers to extend its lines to any place not reached by existing lines, where the inhabitants will advance the cost of building them, the money so advanced to be refunded to the contributors in telegraphing at ordinary tariffs. Under this arrangement a large number of offices have been opened and extensive lines built, to the satisfaction of all parties.

Into such arrangements the government could not enter with any similar rapidity, or by so healthy and economic processes accomplish a like amount of substantial benefit to the people. The fact that there is scarcely a community to be found anywhere in America where the people are unable to meet these offers of the Telegraph Company, is the best reason why government should not furnish at public expense what the people are so able to provide for themselves.

In reply to the statement that our **company** is anxious only for profit, and that its charges are exorbitant as compared with those of other countries, we respectfully call attention to the following table, showing the average cost of telegrams in Europe and America for the year 1866.

AVERAGE COST OF TELEGRAMS IN EUROPE AND **AMERICA** FOR 1866.

Official Statistics of the Telegraphs in Europe for **the Year** 1866.

Name of Country or Company.	Total Number of Messages transmitted, including inland, international, and transit.	Receipts.			Value in U. S. Gold Coin.	Value in U. S. Currency.*
Austria . . .	2,507,472	Florins	1,644,742 ×	$0.48 =	$789,476.16	$1,168,424.71
Belgium . .	1,128,005	Francs	961,112 ×	0.19 =	182,611.28	270,264.69
Bavaria . . .		Florins	322,886 ×	0.41 =	132,383.26	195,927.22
Denmark . .	308,150	Dollars	308,150 ×	1.09 =	335,883.50	497,107.58
France . . .	2,507,472	Francs	7,707,590 ×	0.19 =	1,464,442.10	2,167,374.30
Great Britain and Ireland	5,781,189	£ sterling	512,707 ×	4 86 =	2,491,756.02	3,687,798.90
Italy	1,760,829	Lire	4,120,311 ×	0.19 =	782,859.09	1,158,631.45
Norway . . .	299,375	Dollars	343,645 ×	1.09 =	374,573.15	554,398.26
Prussia . . .	1,964,003	Thalers	1,275,785 ×	0.72 =	918,665.00	1,359,476.20
Russia . . .	838,653	Roubles	1,872,659 ×	0.77½ =	1,451,310.72	2,147,969.86
Switzerland . .	638,916	Francs	684,471 ×	0.19 =	130,049.49	192,473.24
Spain . . .	533,376	Dollars	554,475 ×	1.04½ =	576,654.00	853,447.92
Submarine Telegraph Co. . .	410,760	£ sterling	· 60,368 ×	4.86 =	293,388.48	434,214.95
Malta & Alexandria T. Co.	28,067	£ sterling	52,142 ×	4.86 =	253,410.12	375,046.97
Mediterranean Extension Telegraph Co. . .	77,400	£ sterling	31,200 ×	4.86 =	151,632.00	224,415.36
	18,683,727				$10,328,994.37	$15,286,911.51

Average cost of telegrams in Europe . . . . . 81½ cents.

Statistics of the Western Union Telegraph Company of the United States and of the Montreal Telegraph Company, Dominion of Canada, for the year ending June 30, 1867.

Name of Company.	Total Number of Messages.	Receipts.	United States Currency.
Western Union Telegraph Company	10,067,768†	. . . .	$5,738,627.96
Montreal Telegraph Company	573,219	$258,000 gold =	381,840.00

Average cost of telegrams in the United States . . . . . 57 cents.
Average cost of telegrams in the Dominion of Canada . . . 66 cents.

* **The** Commercial and Financial Chronicle gives the lowest price of gold in 1866 as 124⅞, and the highest 167¾, making the average 148, which we have adopted as the **standard** value for that year.

† **These** are exclusive of railroad messages, of which this company sends many millions per annum. In fact, the safety of all the roads in the United States is largely due to the free use of our wires in running **trains.**

The total receipts of the Western Union Telegraph Company for the above year were $6,568,925.36 ; but of this amount $521,509 were received for transmitting regular press reports on contract, and $308,788.40 from other sources,—leaving only $5,738,627.96 for telegrams.

Of the 10,067,768 messages sent during the year, 8,004,770 were on commercial and social matters, and 2,062,998 containing special press news, the latter amounting to 75,359,670 words.

Of the regular reports there were delivered to the press 294,503,630 words, which, allowing 20 words to each message,—the European standard,—would amount to 14,725,181 telegrams, in addition to the number given in the table. The average telegraphic tolls on these reports were three and one half cents for a message of 20 words, or one and seven tenths of a mill per word.

THE ASSERTED UNION OF THE POSTAL AND TELEGRAPH SYSTEMS IN EUROPE AN ERROR.

In referring to the action of European governments, in their early recognition of the telegraph system, Mr. Washburne says :—

" At once, after the invention and successful establishment of electric telegraphs, every government in Europe where lines were built, except that of Great Britain, established a telegraphic system in connection with its postal system. *Anticipating, as they might well do, that in private hands it might be so constructed as to draw to it, by its speed, safety, and economy, a large proportion of the correspondence, and thus become a rival of the post,* these governments, acting in the interests of the people, have made the system part and parcel of the postal system, and have thrown around it all the safeguards which in every civilized country the postal system enjoys."

The above statement, with the exception of that portion printed in italics, is remarkably incorrect.

In no country in Europe does it appear that the telegraphic administration is connected with the post-office.* In France and Spain the telegraphs are under the control of the Minister of the Interior. In Russia, Prussia, and Italy they belong to the Ministry of Public Works. In Belgium the telegraph, railways, and the post-office form a general division under the Minister of

* Telegraphic Journal, (London: Truscott, Son, & Simmons,) Volume XI. page 131.

Public Works, but are kept distinct. In Austria the administrations of the telegraphs and the post-office were at one time united, but it was found expedient to separate them. In Switzerland the telegraphic organization is nearly the same as Prussia's; the post-office, customs, and private establishments supply the elements of an auxiliary staff, but all the persons employed in the transmission or delivery of telegrams depend on the administration of Telegraphs for their compensation, and in the annual budget an appropriation is made for that service distinct from the post.

An effort was made in France in 1864 to consolidate the post-office and telegraph service, but, owing to the strong opposition evinced on the part of the chief functionaries of both services to such amalgamation, it was relinquished.

It was not until several years after the introduction of the electric telegraph in America that it was opened to the people by any European government. Even in France the electric telegraph was established as late as 1851, and its spread throughout the empire was exceedingly slow. The semaphore telegraph, a defective and inefficient system of conveying intelligence by the exhibition of signals, — introduced by Napoleon at the beginning of the present century, — was still in use, and, notwithstanding the manifest advantages of the electric telegraph, as shown by Arago to the House of Deputies, government long refused to employ it, and, when finally adopted, it was for some time used in connection with the old system.

THE SHORTCOMINGS OF BRITISH TELEGRAPHS.

Mr. Washburne says of the British telegraph :—

" In Great Britain, as in the United States, the telegraph was left to private enterprise and competition. Only a few weeks since, after a twenty years' trial of the system in the hands of private companies, the people of the British islands, with singular unanimity, demanded to have the telegraphic system placed under the control of the postal authorities, and a bill was introduced by the present government for that purpose."

It is complained of Great Britain, which provides one quarter of all the telegraph offices in Europe, that the telegraph companies there have left eighty-eight places in England and Wales having a population of two thousand and upwards, and even whole districts, without an office.

Whatever may be true of the meagreness of the provision of telegraphic facilities by English companies, and which these companies vigorously deny, no such complaint can, with justice, be made in the United States, notwithstanding the vast ranges of territory which must be traversed to meet the communities which need and ask for them.

Without intending any disrespect to the postal authorities of the United States, it may be said that the post-office system of Great Britain, because of the superior character of the control which long and careful study has enabled it to secure, is far in advance of our own. In fact, there is nothing more apparent to an English visitor than the low *status* of our postal arrangements, as compared with that of his own country. It is natural, therefore, seeing the postal system so admirably managed, that English merchants, whose tendencies are all toward governmental direction in matters of this character,* should desire to see the experiment of a similar control of the telegraph. In fact, it is only this class of citizens who have asked for the change, the memorial having gone solely from the different Chambers of Commerce throughout the kingdom, no appeal on the subject having ever been made to or by the people of Great Britain, and therefore the assertion that the people with singular unanimity demanded it is not sustained by the facts.

THE TELEGRAPH SYSTEM OF THE UNITED STATES UNPARALLELED FOR ITS EXTENT AND EFFICIENCY.

Mr. Washburne says, "There is abundant reason to believe that the telegraphic system of Great Britain, which is declared a failure on such high authority, is, in all respects, greatly superior to our own"; but he fails to give any of his reasons for this belief, and we are compelled to assert that it has no intelligent explanation except in a strangely morbid hostility to this company, which exhibits itself on every offered occasion. In all respects the telegraph lines of this country are equal to those of any other, and in some important ones superior. They extend from the Gulf of St. Lawrence to the Gulf of Mexico, and from the Atlantic to the Pacific Ocean, connecting in one unbroken chain more than four

---

* Witness the proposition recently so much discussed in England, that the government should assume control of the railways also.

thousand cities and villages, forming a system by which every event of importance happening in any section of our vast territorial limits is published within a few hours in every other; through which verbatim reports of the speeches in Congress are transmitted from the capital to the metropolis, and full abstracts of them to every considerable town in the nation, on the day of their delivery; which supplies the metropolitan journals with more telegraphic news every day than is contained in the combined press despatches of Europe. Such a system, in its vastness, skilful manipulation, and the rapidity of its unceasing development, we believe merits the public approbation, and is not unworthy of the American name.

Our system of telegraphy is unique. Nowhere else can there be found such an extent of lines under one control. The lines of the Western Union Telegraph Company, extending throughout the United States and portions of the Dominion of Canada, enables it to transmit messages between every section of the country, without undergoing the delay of checking or booking at intermediate points; and between most of the large cities without retransmission. This work, over a territory so vast, although only two years have elapsed since the confederation of lines was effected which made it possible, is fast assuming, under increased care and enlarged experience, the certainty and uniformity of mechanism. In all its effective features, the world may safely be challenged to produce anything to compare with it. The extent of lines and wire belonging to the Western Union Telegraph Company is more than twice that of France, three times greater than that of Prussia, and equals the aggregated systems of Austria, Prussia, and the lesser German States, Italy, Spain, Belgium, and Switzerland, and it is increasing in larger ratio than any European system. The Western Union Telegraph Company alone has added to its lines, during the year 1868, more than five thousand miles of wire, or as much as the entire system of Belgium, leaving unsatisfied demands for an equal extension in the year to come.

ASSERTED EFFECT OF GOVERNMENTAL CONTROL ON BELGIAN TELEGRAPHS.

Mr. Washburne says:—

"In Belgium, where the telegraph has always been under the control of the government, the charge for telegraphing twenty words throughout the kingdom is half a franc, or, say ten cents of our money. In Switzerland the charge is the same. In both these countries offices are opened in nearly every town and village; in both telegraphing is reliable and certain; *complaints of delays and errors are almost unknown, and the lines in both countries yield large profits.**

" In Belgium, in the year 1853, with an average charge of 5 francs and 7 centimes, or say $1.02 for twenty words to any part of the kingdom, the number of messages sent was 52,050, yielding, francs, 265,536. In the year 1866, with the charge reduced to about 17 cents for twenty words, the number of messages had increased to 1,128,005, yielding, francs, 962,213. The same remarkable increase is found in the statistics of the telegraphic system of all countries where the telegraph is under government control."

If by the latter clause of this statement it is designed to convey the idea that government control, *per se*, stimulates the use of the telegraph, or that even a reduction of rates, without this control, is incapable of producing this result, it may justly be challenged as utterly unsustained by the telegraphic experience of this country. The coupling together of these two influences seems designed to prove that the one necessarily involves the other, whereas the question of rate is altogether independent of management, whether government or individual.

EARLY BELGIAN RATES CONTRASTED WITH AMERICAN.

Respecting the Belgian tariff of 1853, of $1.02 in gold per message, for a distance not exceeding fifty miles, it must be regarded as prohibitory, except to those whose necessities compelled its use. The American charge at the same period for even greater distances was twenty-five cents. Instead, therefore, of any surprise at the comparatively limited use of the telegraph by the Belgian people under the circumstances, it may well be regarded as extraordinary that it was used so much.

Had private companies in the United States attempted to impose such a tariff at the period named, public opinion would have compelled an immediate reduction. While there can be no doubt that, within certain limits, a diminished tariff will usually be followed by an increase in the number of messages, experience has demonstrated that this cannot be relied on as invariably true, except

---

* See official acknowledgment of inefficiency on pages 18 and 19; also, on page 96, an admitted loss in performing the service at established rates.

where the charge has been unreasonable or exorbitant. It must be remembered that, when a tariff has been reduced one half, there must be an increase of more than one hundred per cent in the number of despatches, to yield the same revenue, meet the cost of added labor, and provide the necessary additional means of transmission. So great an addition in the number of messages, unattended with a corresponding increase of wires and operators, would result in such delay and inaccuracy as to render the service of no value.

NATURAL INCREASE IN TELEGRAPHY.

It should be remembered, too, that an increase follows the supply of more ample facilities, when these have been inadequate to the wants of the communities for which they are provided.

There is also a large natural increase, altogether irrespective of the charges for transmission, which must be allowed for, before the legitimate effect of the inducements presented by cheapness, or the opportunities furnished by the multiplication of wires or increased capacity in the machinery, can be estimated. Thus, in December, 1848, which in the United States bears a fair comparison with Belgium in 1852 as to date of telegraphic introduction, at the office in Buffalo, N. Y., the receipts amounted to $330.54; while in the same month of 1867, with no decrease in the tariff, the receipts were $5,392.07,—an increase of over 1,600 per cent, and exceeding by 400 per cent that which in Belgium was caused, as claimed, by reducing the tariff from $1.02 to 17 cents, but which, in Buffalo, resulted from simple natural increase caused by the growth of the country and enlarged telegraphic facilities. The annual gross receipts of the Magnetic Telegraph Company, extending between New York and Washington, were as follows : —

1847,	$ 32,810
1848,	52,252
1849,	63,367
1850,	61,383
1851,	67,737
1852,	103,232

Up to the close of 1848 the above company had a monopoly of

the telegraph service between these two cities, but in March, 1849, the House Printing Line commenced operations between New York and Philadelphia, and, together with Bain's Chemical Telegraph, was continued through to Washington in the autumn of that year, so that from 1848 to 1852 the above statement only shows the receipts of one of the three lines doing business between these places. If the receipts of the other two companies were as large, it exhibits the remarkable increase in the amount of business done, in five years, of more than 900 per cent, without any reduction in rates.

The number of messages transmitted by the Magnetic Company in 1852 was 253,857, at an average cost, according to the receipts, of forty cents each.

The average cost of the French telegrams for the same year, according to the official tables furnished by Mr. Washburne, was 11.28 francs, or $2.25 each.

For the year ending November 1, 1868, the Western Union Telegraph Company transmitted over the same territory embraced by the lines of the Magnetic Company in 1852, 1,556,004 messages, the gross receipts upon which were $546,262.05, being an average of thirty-five cents per message. There are two rival companies operating lines between New York and Washington at the present time, so that the comparison between the business for the past year and that of the previous year above given is quite complete.

The gross receipts of the New York and Boston Magnetic Telegraph Association for the year ending

July 31, 1848, were	. . . . .	$34,835.14
" 1853, "	. . . . .	82,214.16
" 1854, "	. . . . .	79,683.73
" 1855, "	. . . . .	101,307.98
" 1856, "	. . . . .	102,151.78
" 1857, "	. . . . .	103,134.06
" 1858, "	. . . . .	98,097.73
" 1859, "	. . . . .	96,136.06

In 1848 the above company had a monopoly of the business between these places, but in 1849 two rival companies constructed lines over this route and divided the business with it.

In 1848 the tariff between New York and Boston was fifty cents for the first ten words, and three cents for each added word; and to intermediate points twenty-five cents for the first ten words, and two cents for each added word.

UNFORTUNATE EFFECTS OF LOW RATES AND COMPETITION.

In 1849 the rate was reduced between New York and Boston to thirty cents, in 1850 to twenty cents, and in 1852 to ten cents. None of the lines, however, paid their working expenses from the time of their construction up to 1853. Even in 1848, when there was no opposition, the expenses exceeded the receipts by $1,199.00. One of the three lines was sold at public auction twice within three years after its construction, to pay the debts incurred in operating it. In 1853 two of the lines were united under one control, and an amicable arrangement entered into between the two remaining companies, by which the rates were advanced approximately to those of 1848, and they remained unchanged for the next ten years.

AMERICAN AND EUROPEAN RATES COMPARED.

In 1851, when the tariff between New York and Boston was twenty cents, the average French rate was $1.56, and the Belgian, for less than one third the distance, $1.56.

In 1852, New York and Boston, tariff,	.	.	.	.	10 cents.
" French, average	"	.	.	.	$2.25 "
" Prussian, "	. "	.	.	.	2.35 "
" Belgian, "	"	.	for less than one third the distance,	1.21 "
" Austrian, "	"	.	.	.	1.55 "
1866, New York and Boston,	"	.	. .	.	.30 "
" French, average,	.	.	.	.	.83 "
" Prussian, "	.	.	.	.	.65 "
" Belgian, "	.	.	for less than one third the distance,	.25 "
" Austrian, "	.	.	.	.	.46 "

When the Belgian lines were opened to the public, an act of the legislature, dated March 15, 1851, established a charge of $2\frac{1}{2}$ francs for a message of twenty words, if transmitted within a circle of 75 kilometres (i.e. 50 cents in gold for a distance of about $46\frac{1}{2}$ miles), and five francs (one dollar gold) for any distance beyond the limit of 75 kilometres.

The increase from 52,050 messages in Belgium in 1853 to 1,128,005 in 1866 is, no doubt, in part justly attributable to the reduction of the prohibitory tariff of the former year, but it is not greater or more remarkable than the increase during the same period in America, where no reduction from the early rates has been made, and where, nevertheless, the business has improved year by year until it has grown into its present volume, exceeding that of any nation on the globe, on whatever basis the comparison be placed.

Belgium transmitted 14,025 messages in 1851 and 52,050 in 1853, being an increase of nearly 400 per cent in three years, although the tariff had been reduced less than 20 per cent. From 1853 to 1862 there· was an increase of over 500 per cent, with a reduction of tariff of about 52 per cent. From 1862 to 1867 there was an increase of less than 400 per cent, although the average tariff had been reduced from 2.07 to 0.85 francs, or about 60 per cent.

Other suggestive illustrations are contained in the tables furnished by Mr. Washburne. Thus, in Switzerland, in 1853, at an average cost of 1.55 francs per message, the number sent was 82,586. In 1854, at an average cost of 1.62 francs, 129,167 were sent, showing an increase of 46,581 messages at a higher tariff. In 1855, when the cost per message was almost identical with that of 1853, the number had increased to 162,851, or about 100 per cent. In 1859, when the cost of messages was 1.48, as compared with 1.35 in 1858, the number had increased from 247,102 to 286,876, and in 1861, at the average charge of 1859, had increased from 286,876 to 333,933. In 1857 and 1862 the charges were exactly alike, yet the increase in the number of messages in the latter year was 113,288, or over 43 per cent over the former. The tables furnished by other countries show similar results. In Prussia, in 1852, 48,751 messages were sent at an average cost of 2.35, while in 1858, at a cost increased to 2.95, 247,292 messages were sent, or an increase of over 400 per cent.

The effect of the policies of the two nations thus shown to be so dissimilar are instructive.

When Belgium, finding it necessary to reduce her tariff to one franc, thereby first attempted to popularize the use of the telegraph, it was done, notwithstanding all its advantages of free rents, absence of taxes, and labor vastly cheaper than in the United States, at a loss to the state of 41,417.19 francs. And when, upon the idea that a still lower tariff might so develop the public use of the lines as to render them self-sustaining, the Belgian government in 1866 reduced the tariff one half, its expenditures were increased thereby from 653,280 francs in 1863 to 1,217,496 francs, entailing a loss of 255,282,000 francs, as shown by Mr. Washburne's report. In the United States, by keeping the tariff at the lowest paying rates, the system has been extended to every part of the country, touching the extreme limits of civilization, and its realm of usefulness is yearly increasing.

THE PECULIARITIES OF THE BELGIAN TELEGRAPH SERVICE.

The telegraph business of Belgium is peculiar. Half of it only can be said to be Belgian at all, the other half being messages in transit, or international, which are sent at comparatively little cost, and for the transmission of which it makes terms with other nations. On the inland or Belgium business proper, the only class which can with any propriety be used in the argument in hand, there was, as has been seen, a loss in 1866 of thirty-four per cent, and in 1867 of thirty-seven and a half per cent. The greater cost of an inland message arises from the fact that it is received, forwarded, and delivered in the kingdom, requiring the various service connected with such duties ; while transit messages simply pass through the state, and impose no expense for labor in transmission, reception, or delivery, and international messages require no delivery in the country sending them.

But besides its annual losses to government, there exists a serious drawback in the value to the people of the reduced tariff. The diminished rate in Belgium is accompanied by no promise of prompt delivery. Despatches at a half-franc each must take their chance of transmission, and submit to the delay caused by other service. Speed rates are established to compensate for loss by the reduced tariff. Thus, a message requiring immediate transit is charged three times an ordinary message, reversing the plan of the Western Union Company, which transmits promptly and indiscriminately at ordinary rates, but makes an immense reduction when the night hours can be used. Of course business men, to whom time is money, are obliged to pay an extra franc to secure that promptness and certainty of transmission without which the telegraph is of little value for all important transactions. The tariff has been, therefore, practically increased to one and a half francs, or forty-two cents for distances which cannot average more than seventy-five miles, and probably do not exceed fifty. The cheap messages take their chance. In America, a repeated message is charged half a rate more than the ordinary tariff. In Belgium it pays four single rates. Cipher messages are also charged four times the price of ordinary messages, while here they are received at ordinary rates.

Were the United States government to construct lines under the Washburne bill, and adopt this Belgian system, its tariffs between Washington and Baltimore — about the average distance of the Belgian service — would be, for prompt delivery such as our telegraph companies perform, *forty-five cents*, instead of the existing charge of ten cents; for messages to which no assurance of promptitude is given, fifteen cents; and for repeated messages, *sixty cents*, instead of our present rate of fifteen cents. If, now, with all its advantages of cheap labor and the profits arising from international and transit messages, the Belgian government, on these bases of charge, admits a clear loss in 1866 of 255,282 francs, how will it be possible for Mr. Washburne to secure a profit to government large enough in a few years to pay the cost of the line, on a common tariff of fifteen cents for all classes of messages?

BELGIAN OFFICIALS ACKNOWLEDGE THE IMPERFECTIONS OF THEIR SYSTEM.

As Mr. Washburne claims for European telegraphs speed, certainty, and economy, it is well to be able to read Belgian official testimony on the same subject. The last report of the Belgian department of public works has the following paragraph: —

" Imperfection has existed at all times and in all places. It is in vain to attempt to obtain equally rapid and exact transmission under all circumstances. **Delay** will occur, whatever may be done to prevent it, **by the blocking up of lines, by** a temporary influx of business; and, **in a** country where distances are short, that delay may equal, and sometimes even exceed, the time that would be occupied in transmitting **by** railway."

Official truthfulness and modesty thus lifts the veil from a system held up for **our** admiration, and reveals its weakness.

INSTRUCTIVE HISTORY OF BELGIAN TELEGRAPHS.

The history of the **use of the telegraph in** Belgium is instructive.

During **1851, the first recorded year of** its existence, there passed between **the offices of** the whole of that kingdom, as shown **by** Mr. **Washburne's** tables, twenty-one messages per day. If we may **suppose, what** seems scarcely credible, **that** only five **of** her chief **cities were** at that time connected by the **wires,** — Ghent, Antwerp, **Brussels,** Bruges, and Liege, — it exhibited the remarkable spectacle **of a** telegraph line opened **by government " in the interest of the people,"** used **to the extent of about four** messages per **day at each of her five** chief cities!

Even after four years more had been used in the extension **of her lines,** the daily transmission only increased to fifty-five messages per day for the whole kingdom, showing how slowly and jealously the **lines** were given to public employment, and how utterly futile **is the** assertion that **the** public interest, at that time at least, **controlled the state in** their management.

The **tariff, which had averaged during the first year $1.26 per** message, and had **not, so far,** been practically **reduced, showed still** more clearly that only the rich used it, and **that it was, on account of its cost,** practically **beyond** the employment **of the people. The truth is, as** Mr. Washburne states, that the Belgian government, **fearing its** use in private hands, and suspicious that by private **energy the** telegraph would be made to rival, if not ruin, the **Belgian** post, seized and held it from popular control. There is **certainly nothing in the** first five years of its existence in Belgium which proves **that** government, **as is** claimed, desired to give the fruits of a great invention to the **Belgian people.** During all of these years, however, and in marked contrast to the lines under government management everywhere, hundreds of thousands of messages were passing over the telegraph lines in the United States, at a tariff which made them available to all its citizens, and showing a daily record in some of the smaller of its inland towns greater than that of all the Belgian offices combined.

When in 1866 the Belgian government, by the radical reduction of the tariff to half a franc, endeavored to render the service more generally useful to the people, it did so at the expense of the public treasury; since on each of the 2,180 inland messages transmitted per day a loss of thirty-eight centimes, or more than two thirds the established rate, was sustained; and, as we have elsewhere stated, this loss would have been much greater, but for a profit derived from international and transit messages, which went to the credit of the whole service.

SINGULAR IDEA THAT A SMALL TELEGRAPH SYSTEM IS MORE DIFFICULT TO MANAGE THAN A LARGE ONE.

"It appears to be tolerably clear," says Mr. Washburne, "that, in order to assert the superiority of a system on a small scale, it requires even more care and greater attention to cope with an increased traffic than an establishment whose ramifications embrace a larger sphere."

This remark is made with reference to the necessity of great promptitude in the delivery of messages in Belgium, where the places connected are contiguous, and conveyance by railroad rapid and frequent. It is made also to show that it is more difficult under such circumstances to cope with an enlarged use of the telegraph than in the United States, where, by reason of distance and the comparative infrequency of transit by railroad, the necessity of promptitude is presumably less urgent.

At first the argument seems fair, but when examined, it has no foundation except in the general fact that distance and infrequent transit by rail may render the telegraph valuable and desirable, even without the promptness essential where transit is rapid and frequent.

The weakness of the argument is evident when it is seen that, as distances decrease, all the elements of cost and maintenance of lines and the difficulties arising from elemental disturbances, lessen in the same proportion. This admits of easy illustration. Look for a moment at Belgium, of which Mr. Washburn treats so copiously. Located centrally in that kingdom, in the form of a triangle, and separated from each other by about thirty miles each, are her three chief cities, Ghent, Brussels, and Antwerp. To connect either two of these a line of telegraph thirty miles long is required, which government builds upon its own property and protects by its own police. However thoroughly built, its cost is necessarily small. There is no trouble or uncertainty in working it. Its very shortness renders its perfection in the use of all the appliances which science and experience have shown desirable readily and cheaply attainable, and it is easily kept in order. When increased public use imperils promptness by the limited provision of wires, ten men, in a single week, can erect another. In all this the very proximity of the points to be connected facilitates and economizes every step required in meeting the enlarged necessities.

The management of such lines, short, well-guarded, and permanent, is almost solely confined to the arrangements for transmission and delivery.

In Belgium, therefore, which contains only two thirds as many offices as the Western Union Telegraph Company maintains in the State of New York alone, with her commercial centres near together, with an average of less than three wires on her poles, with her 2,232 miles of line on government property and protected by its authority, want of promptness would be inexcusable, because so easily effected. Were New York and Chicago only thirty miles apart, and all the messages of the United States, now approximating thirteen millions per annum, required to be passed between them at the rate of 36,000 per day, and within an average of fifteen minutes from the time of their reception, as is now done between the Chambers of Commerce of these cities, it could be accomplished with comparative ease, and especially so were the land which the wires traversed the property of the company, and the lines guarded by the nation. Once render it easy and inexpensive to provide a reliable outward structure, and the work of the telegraph becomes a matter of simple internal organization, except as competition and the necessities of extension in a land so vast as ours adds to the ordinary cares of administration. The immense distances between our centres of commerce, the multitude of far separated radiating centres of business, the great exposure and defective protection of our lines, and constantly increasing system of wires which are constructed as rapidly as new demands for their extension are made, render the management of this company one of the most arduous and complicated of private enterprises. There is nothing in Europe or elsewhere which bears any proper resemblance to the American telegraph system, nor with which it can be properly compared.

Between the systems of Belgium and the United States we witness the following marked contrast. The companies here have only one tariff for transmission, and all take their turn. The payment of an extra franc cannot, as in Belgium, purchase priority, or give one advantage over his neighbor. This is an imposition of the government, similar to, and even less defensible, than that which in England requires four postages to secure the safety of a letter. Here the companies offer to guarantee the public against error by an extra payment of one half the ordinary tariff; but the public, because of their confidence in the company, do not avail themselves of this provision to an extent of one in ten thousand! Messages sent in cipher, for which no extra charge is made in the United States, can only be sent in Europe by the payment of four ordinary tariffs, and in some states in Europe, and among others France, the government will not permit their being sent at all.

NECESSITY FOR THE UNIFICATION OF THE TELEGRAPH SYSTEM.

It is curious to observe that the reasons assigned for the advantages to be gained by governmental control are precisely the same which led to the consolidation under one management of the great mass of the American lines, and which has led to the unjust charge of monopoly as the work of unification has progressed.

Mr. Scudamore says: "When I began to collect the information on which this report is based, I was not free from doubts as to the propriety of the scheme; but, after patiently collecting and considering all the data which I could obtain, I found myself driven, by the mere force of facts, to the conclusion at which I have arrived. This conclusion, indeed, is almost identical with that to which the directors of the Electric and International Telegraph Company came in the year 1852, and which they thus stated to their stockholders : —

" The delays, inaccuracies, and expense of the continental telegraphs are an exemplification of the great advantage to the public of the administration *being under a single management. This circumstance alone admits of the establishment of a low and uniform tariff.* . . . . The telegraph has already become a most powerful and useful agent, and has, in a measure, been adopted as a means of communication by persons employed in commercial pursuits, but, owing to the want of proper arrangement and facilities, and the fact of the management of the lines being divided *by several companies,* without unison in action or interest, the public generally have been debarred from benefiting by the immense accommodation and advantages the telegraph is capable of affording."

In presenting the same idea, Mr. Washburne, with a looseness of statement for which we know of no proper justification, remarks as follows : —

"There can be no doubt that the superiority of the continental system over every other is due to the fact that the telegraph there is a government institution, while in this country it is left to private enterprise. Individual and associated effort have done much, but, with the confusion of our telegraphic system before us, it would be folly to shut our eyes to the inherent weakness of all joint-stock enterprises. Absence of responsibility, waste of labor, irresolute councils, expensive management, want of effective control over subordinates, are among the evils of such associations, to say nothing of the imperative demands of stockholders that dividends shall be made and that none shall be hazarded. Under government control one governing body would do the work now done by twenty, and the obligation to realize profits would not interfere to prevent the reduction of rates or the proper extension of the system."

Passing over the charges of " waste, irresponsibility, and irresolute councils," which serve to round the paragraph in which they occur, the focal idea is the efficiency secured by a united control. That is the very basis of this company's organization. Discarding as false and perilous any general assumption of the enterprises of the people by the government, and accepting its refusal to attach the telegraph to its administration, when offered to it by its inventor, as for the best interest of the nation, this company early saw that united action between the extremes of our territorial limits was as essential to its own success as to public convenience. With numerous companies, of limited jurisdiction, and tariffs on all bases, — which had to be added and dovetailed to each other whenever a despatch passed between two distant places, — there was neither certainty of correctness, promptitude, nor the possibility of a low and uniform tariff. To secure all of these the leading telegraph organizations combined. It was a step necessary alike for public usefulness and success, and is accomplishing all that could be desired. The system has penetrated farther, and compassed more territory than separate organizations could have attempted or than even government itself would have been willing to undertake. Its administration is vast, harmonious, liberal, exact, economical, and just. It uses its revenues largely to extend its realm of usefulness to the people of every section of the country. It seeks to secure the highest skill and character in its employees. Its aim is to give the wires to the use of the whole people on the lowest terms consistent with proper self-support and the just return which capital and skill demand. It will accomplish all the nation requires of it, if allowed to solve its own problem, making the wires the accepted right arm of the public industries, and the emblem of universal unity and good-will.

ESTIMATE OF THE COST OF BUILDING TELEGRAPH LINES.

Mr. Washburne says : —

"Any one at all familiar with the prices of materials and labor in the various countries will see that, as to materials for the construction of lines, they are cheaper here than in any European country, and that the whole cost of constructing telegraphic lines must be less here than in Belgium or Switzerland. In the latter country a large proportion of the lines are erected upon iron posts, the prime cost of which with the stone base is from $6 to $9 each, or from five to seven times the cost of the posts usually employed in America.

" As to the exact cost of constructing lines in the United States it is difficult to procure reliable data. There are few questions apparently so simple upon which so many conflicting opinions have been printed. So simple a matter as the cost of posts, say thirty feet long, the placing of them in the earth, furnishing and placing the necessary iron wires and insulators and the fitting up of stations with instruments and furniture, ought not, one would suppose, to be a difficult thing to fix. Yet persons claiming to be experts, and even authorities in all matters relating to telegraphs, have differed very widely. **Mr.** Prescott, a telegraph superintendent, and the author of a work on ' Electric Telegraphs,' estimates the cost of a mile of telegraph, built as they ordinarily are, at $ 61.80.* . . .

" This is about the cost of construction of a majority of our lines, but if built as they should be, they would cost $ 150 per mile. If additional wires are added, each wire put up would be, per mile, $ 32.80."

Mr. Washburne's statement, that telegraph lines can be built cheaper in the United States than in Europe, is entirely incorrect. Labor, wire, machinery, insulators, and every appliance peculiar to the telegraph, are very much cheaper in Europe than in America, and large importations of wire are constantly being made from Belgium and England, notwithstanding the heavy duty.

The difference in the cost of labor in Europe and America is very great. The most recent authentic publication on the subject † states that the general average rates paid for all kinds of labor in the United Kingdom are as follows : For adult males, in England, $ 4.96 per week ; in Scotland, $ 4.52 ; in Ireland, $ 3.16. For boys and youths, under twenty years of age, in England, $ 1.44 ; in Scotland, $ 1.70 ; in Ireland, $ 1.38. For adult women, in England, $ 2.76 ; in Scotland, $ 2.32 ; in Ireland, $ 2.06. For girls, under twenty years of age, in England, $ 1.88 ; in Scotland, $ 1.80 ; in Ireland, $ 1.62. These rates are stated to be high, as compared with other countries in Europe.

In Belgium, coal-miners earn from 33 cents to $ 1.00 per day, the average being 56 cents. In iron-furnaces, a puddler earns from 92 cents to $ 1.10, and the under hands from 50 cents to 62 cents per day. In iron-foundries, a moulder earns from 44 cents to 62 cents per day. In Paris, the average for adult male labor is 76 cents per day, and for women 38 cents; but in the interior of France the price is much less. In Prussia, first-class engineers earn $ 1.10, and second-class 83 cents.

Among the working classes in the United Kingdom are in-

---

* This statement was written in 1859, and the object of the author was to show the inferior manner in which a majority of the lines were constructed at that time.

† **Wages** and Earnings of the Working Classes. By Leone Levi, F. S. S., F. S. A., Professor of the Principles and Practice of Commerce in King's College. London : John Murray. 1867.

cluded all who, whether as workers for others or as workers for themselves, are employed in manual labor, be it productive of wealth or not; and they are divided into five classes, viz. professional, domestic, commercial, agricultural, and industrial. The total number of workers is estimated at eleven millions, and the average weekly earnings in the United Kingdom are: Men, under twenty, $1.59; from twenty to sixty, $4.18; women, under twenty, $1.72; from twenty to sixty, $2.41. Average weekly earnings from every avocation in Great Britain and Ireland, $3.16.

Thirty per cent of the people of the United Kingdom live in houses the rental of which is less than $31 per annum, and seventeen per cent in those under $45 per year.

In the preparation of the following table we have consulted Professor Levi's work on Wages and Earnings in England; "Government and the Telegraphs" (London, 1868); "Special Report on the Electric Telegraph Bill"; "Publications of the Statistical Bureau at Washington"; and the official records of the Western Union Telegraph Company.

Statement showing the Average Cost of Labor in England and the United States.

Prices paid per Day.	England.	United States.
Carpenters and Builders......................	$1.14	$3.25
Dock Laborers..............................	.68	2.25
Engineers.................................	1.32	3.85
Farm Laborers.............................	.42	2 00
Iron Founders.............................	1.10	3.25
Moulders..................................	1.25	3.50
Letter-Carriers *..........................	.74	2.18
Printers	1.02	2.50
Policemen.................................	.85	3.00
Railroad Conductors	.92	3.85
Soldiers...................................	.22	.62
Servant-girls	.16	.48
Telegraph Employees †.....................	.41	1.29

* The number of letter carriers employed by the British Post-Office Department for the year 1866 was 11,449, and the total expenditures for the same $2,664,000, being an average of $232.68 per annum for each man.

The number of letter-carriers employed by the Post-Office Department of the United States for the year 1866 was 863, and the total expenditures for the same $589,236.41, being an average of $682.77 for each man.

† The cost of labor of telegraph employees is obtained by dividing the total amount paid for labor by the number of persons employed of all kinds. The average price per day for operators in the United States is $2.25, and in England 62 cents.

With a knowledge of the great difference in the cost of labor and material in Europe and America which the above statistics show, we cannot comprehend the propriety of Mr. Washburne's assertion that the whole cost of constructing telegraphic lines must be less here than in Belgium or Switzerland.

Even our poles are purchased in the Dominion of Canada, and paid for in gold. The cost of transportation from the St. Lawrence to New York cannot be much, if any, more than the cost of their delivery at London, Havre, or Brussels.

In the United States, telegraph-poles are of cedar or chestnut, — more generally of the former. In England, the larch is the most common; in Russia, the pine; in France, pine, alder, poplar, and other white woods; and in Germany, spruce and pine.*

The cost of a telegraph line depends, like the cost of a house or any other structure, upon how it is built, but Mr. Washburne, or any other intelligent man, ought to know that the price appropriated in his bill for a four-wire line from Washington to New York cannot possibly build it, even should government build such a structure as those which a dozen years ago cursed the enterprise, and made it a reproach and shame. When government builds a line of telegraph on the plea of public necessity, it should require that its structures at least be equal to those of its citizens. It is not strange that, with the crude and cheap ideas formed by Mr. Washburne of telegraph structures, he disparages and undervalues the properties of the existing companies, and ridicules the estimates furnished Congress in their communications.

DOUBTS REGARDING THE ESTIMATES OF TELEGRAPH EXPERTS AS TO COST OF CONSTRUCTING LINES.

We quote from Mr. Washburne's paper: —

"In February, 1866, when, in view of the establishment of an experimental government line of telegraph, the Postmaster-General was called upon for information 'in regard to the feasibility and usefulness of establishing. in connection with the Post-Office Department, telegraph lines,' &c., 'to be opened to the public at minimum rates of charge, ... and such statistics and exhibits predicated on cost of construction and capacity of transmission as will best illustrate its practica-

* Telegraph Manual.

bility,' he sent to Congress lengthy statements, all of them prepared by persons believed to be interested in or officers of existing companies, in which the cost of a telegraphic line with six wires is put down by one writer at $1,400 per mile, by others at $665, exclusive of river cables and lines through cities.

"Among other statements so furnished is an amended one by Mr. Prescott, whose statement, when made part of a work intended as authority in telegraphic matters, is quoted above. For reasons not explained his views underwent a marked change between 1860 and 1866, and he makes haste to refute his own previous statements. His revised statement is as follows: —

"'It is well known by every person who has any knowledge of telegraphy in this country previous to the publication of my work in 1860, that comparatively few lines had been at that time even tolerably well constructed; and one object which I had in view in writing it was to call attention to this prevailing fault, and endeavor to get a better system inaugurated.

"'Since then there has been a very marked improvement in the construction of telegraph lines in this country. Small poles, of inferior wood, which required renewing every few years, have given place to large and more enduring ones of chestnut and cedar, and small iron wire, which offered great resistance to the passage of the electric current, has given place to zinc-coated wire of larger size and greater conductivity.

"'But while the quality of the lines has greatly improved under the experienced and liberal management of the telegraph companies, the cost of constructing lines has kept pace with the increased cost of everything else, and has more than doubled within the past six years, so that lines which could have been built in 1860 for $150 per mile could not now be constructed for *twice that amount*. A substantial telegraph line, constructed on the line of a railroad, with *cedar* or *chestnut* poles thirty feet in length, and six inches at the top by twelve at the butt, set forty to the mile, with most improved form of insulator and best galvanized wire, would cost $400 per mile for a single wire. If forty-foot poles were used (which would be necessary if many wires were to be placed upon one set of poles), it would cost $600 per mile for a single wire. When fifty-foot poles are used, the cost is very greatly enhanced.

"'Mr. Brown estimates the total cost of all the telegraph property in the United States at "a little more than $2,000,000." Now, if we estimate the present cost of the lines and their equipment at the moderate price of $300 per mile, and the number of miles of wire in the country at only 150,000, we have a total cost of $45,000,000, without reckoning the value of the patents, franchises, &c.

"'Mr. Brown states that "telegraphs properly constructed, the timber well prepared and wire protected, will last for 20 years." This may be true, but it remains to be proved.'"

We fail to discern any refutation by Mr. Prescott of his previous statements. His reasons for a change in the estimates for building a telegraph line in 1866 over those of 1860 hardly need be stated. If the results of the intervening years of civil war, by which a million of able-bodied men were cut off from the fields of labor, the industries of the country burdened with enormous taxes before unknown, and prices inflated by the issue of hundreds of millions of paper **dollars, do not suggest them, there is small** hope of profit from **the practical lessons of the times.**

INCORRECT ASSERTION THAT AMERICAN TELEGRAPHS ARE NOT CONSTRUCTED ACCORDING TO SPECIFICATIONS.

Mr. Washburne says : —

"The officers of the telegraph companies, whose elaborate statement is also forwarded by the Postmaster-General, estimate as follows : —

" ' Cost of construction, including engineering, patents, and franchises, **per** mile : one wire — six wires.

" ' The cost of building lines varies according to locality, timber, method, nature of the ground, and the wires to be borne.

" ' A line from New York to Washington should be of the best class, and would be represented by the following figures : —

43 poles delivered **at stations,**	$161.25
129 **arms,** complete,	129.00
43 **holes,** five feet deep, tools, &c.,	30.00
Labor, — handling, preparing, erecting, &c.,	25.00
Six wires, at twelve cents per pound,	240.00
Labor, — wiring, transportation, &c.,	30.00
Distributing poles,	25.00
Superintendence, &c.,	25.00
	665.25

240 miles at $665.25, Washington to New York,	$159,660
Lines through New York, Philadelphia, Baltimore, **and Washington,**	16,000
22 cables at rivers south of the Hudson,	20,000
Cable at Hudson River, house, boats, &c.,	8,000
	$203,660

" ' The cost of franchises and patents cannot be given.

" ' Such a line built by government, carefully, and with reference **to per-**manence, with six wires, would cost $250,000.

" ' If, however, it is seriously contemplated by the **government** to construct lines along the great **commercial** routes, and if it be the design in so doing to remove from the system, by every attainable appliance or improvement, all its ascertained defects, a structure of larger poles, and wires of superior conducting qualities, will be built. Such a line should be constructed of the most solid and durable wood, such as the black locust, so that masses of sleet or moist snow, so destructive to present lines, would leave it uninjured. Heavier wires also, **which,** by their increased conducting capacity, would give greater facility and **certainty** to transmission, should be used.

" ' **These** improvements, with greater **care** taken in the execution of the work **than in** that of ordinary structures, will, of course, increase its cost in proportion **to the care** bestowed. And should the government determine to provide facil-**ities equal** to those now proffered by private companies, it would be necessary to erect **at least** five lines of poles bearing six wires each, that being the number (thirty in all) now in use between New York and Washington by all the companies.

" ' A common wire line, intended to bear one, and not more than two wires, can be built for $ 150 to $ 180 per mile, the wire being number nine, galvanized, the poles of limited size, and costing not over $ 1.25 each.'

" It nowhere appears that such lines as all these writers insist shall be built by the government have ever been built in this or any other country. They seem to have taken it as matter of course that the government, if the experiment proposed should be tried, will depart from the usual method of construction and build the novel and costly structures for which their estimates are made. One looks in vain in the communication sent to Congress by the Postmaster-General for any reliable information as to the cost of a telegraphic line, constructed as such lines are in this and other countries, and such a line as the government, if it should be determined to build an experimental line, would probably build."

COST OF AMERICAN TELEGRAPHS ESTIMATED BY EUROPEAN DATA.

In reply to Mr. Washburne's statement that no such lines as all these writers insist shall be built by the government have ever been built in this or any other country, we respectfully, but firmly, assert that he is mistaken. This company possesses thousands of miles of telegraph lines constructed after the specifications given above, and costing as much as the estimates which he so emphatically distrusts. In order, however, to set this matter of cost at rest, we will endeavor to establish it by comparison with those of all other countries of which we have been able to procure official data.

Mr. Frank Ives Scudamore, one of the assistant secretaries of the British Post-Office, and the gentleman who furnished the reports and data by which the British government were induced to monopolize the telegraph in that country, and who shows no disposition to overvalue the property or services of private telegraph companies, testified before the select committee of the House of Commons, July 9, 1868, that the total number of miles of telegraph in operation in Great Britain in 1866 was 16,000, and that the companies expended in constructing the same about £2,300,000.*

The capital stock of the various companies represented a larger sum than this, and Mr. Scudamore himself acknowledges that he

* Special Report, Electric Telegraph Bill, ordered by the House of Commons to be printed, 16 July, 1868. See testimony on pages 149 and 150.

has got the amount under the mark rather than over it; therefore we presume that Mr. Washburne will allow this to be a fair estimate. Now £2,300,000 sterling is equal to $11,132,000 in gold, or $16,475,360 in United States legal money. This sum, divided by 16,000 miles of line, gives us $1,029.71 as the cost per mile.

The Belgian system comprised, at the end of 1866, 3,519 kilometres of telegraph lines, equal to 2,187 English miles. The cost of constructing these lines, up to December, 1866, amounted to 2,055,083 francs, equal to $411,016.60 gold, or $608,304.56 currency; which would give $274.14 for each mile of line. It must be borne in mind, however, that the Belgian government, owning all the railroads, could transport all the telegraph material free, and in many other ways greatly reduce the cost of the lines; of course the right of way cost them nothing, and with us this is an important item.

Bavaria has 2,115 miles of line, which cost for construction 843,207 florins, equal to $340,092.28 gold, or $503,338.35 in our currency. This would make the cost per mile $240. The same conditions, however, which reduced the cost of construction in Belgium tended to the same result in Bavaria.

In France there are 20,028 miles of lines costing 23,800,791 francs, equal to $4,760,158.20 in gold, or $7,045,034.13 in currency, making the average cost of each mile of line $351.75.

RECAPITULATION.

Average cost per mile of telegraph line in Great Britain and Ireland,	$1,029.71
Average cost per mile of telegraph line in Belgium,	274.14
" " " " " " Bavaria,	240.00
" " " " " " France,	351.75
Total cost of telegraphs in Great Britain and Ireland,	$16,475,360.00
" " " " Belgium,	608,304.56
" " " " Bavaria,	503,338.35
" " " " France,	7,045,034.13
Total cost for the four countries,	$24,632,637.04

Total number of miles of telegraph line in Great Britain and
Ireland, ... 16,000
Total number of miles of telegraph line in Belgium, . . 2,187
"   "   "   "   "   Bavaria, . . . 2,115
"   "   "   "   "   France, . . 20,028

Total number of miles of telegraph in the four countries, 40,330
Average cost of construction of each mile of telegraph line for
the four countries above named, ... $610.76

VALUE OF WESTERN UNION TELEGRAPH PROPERTY, BASED ON EUROPEAN DATA.

The number of miles of line belonging to this company is 50,760, and the number of miles of wire is 97,416.

Taking the average cost per mile of telegraph line in England as a basis for a calculation of the cost of the lines of the Western Union Telegraph Company, we have a total value of $52,166,079.60. If we estimate the cost of our lines by the average cost of all the telegraph lines in Europe of which any statistics can be obtained, we have a total value of $31,002,177.60.

Much has been said respecting the alleged unreasonably large capital of the Western Union Telegraph Company. This company was organized in the year 1851, with a capital of three hundred and sixty thousand dollars, and constructed a line of electric telegraph from Buffalo, N. Y., to Louisville, Ky., distance about six hundred miles. The cost of the line, on a gold basis, was thus $600 per mile. The present extent of line belonging to this company, if estimated by the cost of the original line, and forty per cent be added for the premium on gold, would give us $42,638,400 as its value. On the basis of the cost of the lines of the Atlantic and Pacific Telegraph Company, the capital of the Western Union Telegraph Company would be about $100,000,000, and, on that of some other rival lines, nearly $200,000,000.

The gross receipts of the Western Union Telegraph Company from July 1, 1866, to November 1, 1868, — two years and four months, — were $16,088,498.86, and the gross expenses $9,862,272.31 ; leaving $6,226,225.75 as the net earnings, being an average of over seven per cent per annum on the capital of the company, which is $40,347,700. After applying $1,934,040.61 of the receipts of the past two years towards the construction of new lines, and the redemption of the bonds of the company, it has made, with one exception, regular semiannual dividends of two per cent. Such a property as this, if situated in England, or any other country in Europe, would be regarded as so valuable that its stock would be held at par, and yet it is selling in our markets at the present time at sixty-four per cent discount, or at thirty-six dollars per share! At this price the entire property, including payment of the bonded debt, would only cost $19,415,672.

Now what is the explanation of this singular distrust of the value of this great property as shown by its insignificant present market value? Less than four years ago the stock sold at above par, and its earnings and prospects were then inferior to what they are at the present time. An examination of the tables on page 39 will show that the gross receipts and net earnings have constantly increased during the past two and a half years, and there is every reason, so far as the management and prosperity of the company is concerned, why its market value should have increased instead of depreciating. The explanation for this singular state of things is to be found in the constant agitation in Congress of various schemes for the construction and operation of government telegraphs, at prices very much lower than the cost of the service. Let any industry be thus constantly menaced, and it must necessarily suffer in public estimation as a safe investment. We trust the subject will be effectually settled during the present session of Congress, and the incubus which has so long rested upon this important enterprise be removed.

ERRONEOUS ESTIMATE OF THE VALUE OF THE WESTERN UNION TELEGRAPH COMPANY'S PROPERTY.

Mr. Washburne says : —

" The statement furnished by the officers of the telegraph companies, for the information of the Postmaster-General, and by him forwarded to Congress as his reply to the call for information, is well calculated to remove all doubts as to the value of this kind of property. Among other items of information is the following : —

" ' The length of wire owned by the Western Union and United States companies is 60,000 miles.* The average cost, as based on the now united capital, is $450 per mile. This embraces, besides the poles, wires, and apparatus, the following : —

Invested in buildings,	$95,208.83
Stocks in other companies,	1,429,900.00
Office fittings,	360,000.00

"It is remarkable that while *the length of wire* is given, the length of line nowhere appears.† There is a vast difference between the cost of a *telegraph line* and a *telegraphic wire*. We have seen the cost of a line with a single wire estimated at $61.80, and each additional wire placed on the same posts, $31.80 per mile.

"In the absence of any exact information on the subject, we may fairly estimate that the lines of the companies named average three wires to each line. They possess, then, 20,000 miles of telegraph line, with an average of three wires thereon. They speak of 'single wire lines costing $180 per mile.' This estimate is too high for any line now in use ; but if it be adopted as the basis of calculation, and an allowance of $45 per mile be made for each additional wire, we have, for the 20,000 miles of line owned by the companies named, a cost of $5,400,000, represented by a capital stock of $41,000,000 ! 'The average cost' per mile of each wire suspended on their lines, '*as based on the now united capital*, is $450 per mile.' If 'the united capital' had been based upon the actual cost of the property of the company, it would have been nearer $4,000,000 than $41,000,000.

"The 'information' furnished to the Postmaster-General is compiled with the evident intent to discourage the experiment then contemplated. It is incomplete, and is compiled with an intent to mislead. To any one who will take the trouble to examine it carefully, and to apply the proper tests to its assertions, it furnishes additional arguments in favor of a careful experiment by the government in the construction and maintenance of telegraph lines under control of the Post-Office Department."

To impugn the motives of an opponent is the weakest of arguments. If his statements are wrong, it is easy to show wherein, but wholesale denunciation convinces no one of the strength of the cause or the culpability of the assailed. We do not question Mr. Washburne's honesty of purpose in making his unjust and extremely erroneous statements regarding the property or executive ability of the Western Union Telegraph Company, but we do say that he is most egregiously deceived upon all points which he has discussed.

In reply to the charges which Mr. Washburne brings against

* This estimate was made before the consolidation of the American Telegraph Company and other properties with the Western Union Telegraph Company, and when its capital was only $27,000,000.

† We have given the length of the lines, as well as the length of the wires belonging to the Western Union Telegraph Company, on page 32.

the Western Union **Telegraph Company, of** compiling information for the Postmaster-General with an intent to mislead, of exaggerating the cost **of construction of lines,** and misrepresenting the value **of its** own, we respectfully present the following facts respecting **the** organization of the company, the amount of its capital, the number of miles of line and the number of miles of **route,** together **with a** statement of the number of skilled persons **in its** employ.

THE ORGANIZATION OF THE WESTERN UNION TELEGRAPH COMPANY.

In the spring of 1866 there were **three** telegraph companies, covering vast areas **of territory in the** United States. Two **of** these companies **operated lines over** separate divisions of **the** country, **but worked** in connection with each other, while the third, which covered some portions of the territory of the others, was **a** competitor for the business of all sections. These three **companies** were the Western Union, with lines extending from **New** York to California, and throughout the Western States ; the American, with lines extending **from** the Gulf of the **St. Lawrence to** the Gulf of Mexico, **and through** the **lower Mississippi and** Ohio Valleys ; **and** the United States, with **lines extending from** Portland, Me., to Richmond, **Va.,** and from **New** York **to Kansas.**

The necessity for direct communication between the East and **the** West, and the **economy** of one set of officers and employees instead of **two,** demanded the consolidation of the American and the Western **Union ;** and the still greater saving **to** all the companies by the **uniting of** the lines **and** offices of the United States with those of **the other** two equally **necessitated its** amalgamation with the others.

	Par Value.	Market Value.
The capital **of** the Western Union Telegraph Company, which had sold at par **and** over in 1865, was	$ 22,000,000	$ 22,000,000
The capital stock of the American **Telegraph** Company, which sold **at $ 180** per share in 1865, was	4,000,000	7,200,000
The **capital** stock of the United States Telegraph Company was	11,000,000	11,000,000
	$ 37,000,000	$ 40,200,000

The proportion of lines and wires to the capital varied with each company, the American company having the greater number; and in the terms of consolidation these differences were equitably arranged, and the capital stock of the consolidated company was established as follows : —

FINANCIAL STATISTICS OF THE WESTERN UNION TELEGRAPH COMPANY.

CAPITAL STOCK.

At the date of the Report of October, 1865, the capital stock of the company issued was	$21,355,100
It has since been increased as follows: —	
October, 1865, by conversion of bonds	500
November, 1865 by exchange for stock of California State Telegraph Company	122,500
December, " by exchange for Lodi Telegraph Stock	500
" " by exchange for Trumansburg and Seneca Falls Telegraph Stock, . . .	3,500
" " by issue to Hicks & Wright for Repeater Patent, ...	1,500
" " by exchange for Missouri and Western Telegraph Stock, ...	400
" " by exchange for House Telegraph Stock,	1,400
April, 1866, by 2½ per cent Stock Dividend, to equalize stock as per Consolidation Agreements,	472,300
" by consolidation with United States Telegraph Company, ...	3,845,800
June, " by issue for United States Pacific Lines,	3,333,300
July, " by consolidation with American Telegraph Company, ...	11,818,800
" " by exchange for P. C. & L. Telegraph Stock, ...	4,100
December 1, 1867, by fractions converted, to date, . .	49,100
Total present capital, ...	$41,008,800

Of the stock issued for United States Pacific Lines there was returned to the company, as consideration for completing construction of Pacific Line, ...	$883,300	
The company owns also, ...	120,800	
	$1,004,100	

Out of this we have issued for —

Southern Express Co.'s Telegraph Lines,	$ 150,000	
California State Telegraph Co.'s Stock,	124,700	
Other Telegraph Lines,	80,000	
		354,700

Now owned by the company, ... 649,400

Balance, on which we are liable for dividends, . $ 40,359,400

BONDED DEBT.

Bonds of the American Telegraph Company, due in 1873, . $ 89,500

Bonds of the Western Union Telegraph Company, due in 1875, ... 4,857,300

Total Bonded Debt, December 1, 1867, . . . $ 4,946,800

The greater portion of the debt of the Western Union Telegraph Company was incurred in the grand attempt to construct a line on the Northwest Coast, and across Behrings Strait to connect with the Russian line at the mouth of the Amoor River, known as Collins's Overland Line to Europe, which was abandoned on the successful submergence and operation of the Atlantic Cable.

The financial condition of the Western Union Telegraph Company May 1, 1868, was as follows : —

CAPITAL STOCK.

At the date of the Report of January 1, 1868, the Capital Stock of the Company, issued, was, . . . $ 41,008,800.00

It has since been increased as follows : —

By exchange for United States Telegraph Stock,	$ 10,800.00	
By exchange for American Telegraph Stock,	2,400.00	
By exchange for House Telegraph Stock,	100.00	
By fractions converted,	600.00	
		13,900.00

Total Capital Stock issued May 1, 1868, . . 41,022,700.00

Of this there is owned by the Company, . . 675,000.00

Balance on which dividends are payable, . . $ 40,347,700.00

BONDED DEBT.

Bonds outstanding December 1, 1867, ...	$ 4,946,800.00
Bonds of 1875 since purchased and cancelled, . . .	56,300.00
Balance of Bonded Debt May 1, 1868, . .	$ 4,890,500.00

Maturing as follows: In 1873, . .	$ 89,500.00	
In 1875, . .	4,801,000.00	
		$ 4,890,500.00

PROPERTY ACCOUNT.

Telegraph Lines and Property, December 1, 1867,	.	$ 47,733,640.68
Since added,		
By exchange of Stocks, as per Stock Account, ...	$ 13,300.00	
By Application of Profits:—		
Construction Account, . $ 103,592.13		
Purchase of Telegraph Stocks, 23,806.66		
Purchase of Real Estate, . 3,011.14		
———— $ 130,409.93		
	$ 143,709.93	
Total Property Account, May 1, 1868, .	.	$ 47,877,350.61

STOCK, BOND, AND PROPERTY BALANCES, MAY 1, 1868.

	Assets.	Liabilities.
Telegraph Lines, Equipment, Franchises, etc., ...	$ 47,051,358.49	
Western Union Telegraph Stock owned by Company, ...	667,342.50	
Productive Stock in other Telegraph Companies, ...	52,471.81	
Real Estate, ...	106,177.81	
Capital Stock, ...		$ 41,022,700.00
Fractional Shares, ...		15,110.00
Bonded Debt, ...		4,890,500.00
Bond and Mortgage, Buffalo Property,		15,000.00
Profits used for Purchase of Property, and Redemption of Bonds, . .		1,934,040.61
	$ 47,877,350.61	$ 47,877,35.061

STATEMENT OF INCOME AND EXPENSES FROM JULY 1, 1866, TO NOVEMBER 1, 1868.

1866.	Gross Receipts.	Expenses.	Net Profits.
July,	$ 562,292.97	$ 410,382.40	$ 151,910.57
August,	548,716.96	346,742.31	201,974.65
September,	556,955.95	298,931.99	258,023.96
October,	623,528.31	344,245.07	279,283.24
November,	571,036.02	322,508.66	248,527.36
December,	551,971.40	302,596.41	249,374.99
January,	580,560.53	341,104.71	239,455.82
February,	483,441.77	314,617.26	168,824.51
March,	530,642.66	297,076.59	233,566.07
April,	545,586.30	320,869.41	224,716.89
May,	525,437.94	326,829.83	198,608.11
June,	488,754.55	318,100.99	170,653.56
July,	536,156.89	360,917.53	175,239.36
August,	570,676.85	375,970.17	194,706.68
September,	601,548.79	375,641.50	225,907.29
October,	628,836.74	393,459.92	235,376.82
November,	583,723.66	370,429.57	213,294.09
December,	576,135.19	379,291.35	196,843.84
1868.			
January, .	539,794.00	366,446.02	173,347.98
February,	600,183.32	345,855.52	254,327.80
March,	587,962.23	335,947.64	252,014.58
April,	602,257.05	356,349.18	245,907.87
May,	597,374.47	349,165.41	248,209.06
June,	579,911.00	353,375.50	226,535.50
July,	601,730.61	396,163.66	205,566.95
August,	602,304.73	376,452.03	225,852.70
September,	630,665.36	372,197.50	258,467.86
October,	680,311.81	410,604.17	269,707.64
	$ 16,088,498.86	$ 9,862,272.31	$ 6,226,225.75

STATIONS, LINES, AND EMPLOYEES OF THE WESTERN UNION TELEGRAPH COMPANY.

The Western Union Telegraph Company alone has

3,331 Telegraph Offices,
50,760 Miles of Line,
97,416 Miles of Telegraphic Wire,
265 Submarine Cables,
6,389 Skilled persons in its employ.

ENGLISH AND AMERICAN TELEGRAPHS COMPARED.

It has been shown that, several years before there is any record of regular public telegraph business in continental Europe, the system in the United States was in popular use. There can be no question that what restrained its use in Europe for so many years was governmental jealousy of its power, and not ignorance of its capacity. The subject was freely canvassed in the public prints, and was familiar to the learned men of all European nations. Even in England, whose government aided its introduction through private enterprise, the employment of the telegraph was hindered by a tariff so high as to shut it out from general use. Respecting this latter fact, so as to give in more marked contrast the early history of the telegraph on the two continents, a few details are given.

The Electric Telegraph Company of England was incorporated in 1846, and seems to have made its first work in the connection of the railway stations, post-office, police, admiralty, Houses of Parliament, Buckingham Palace, &c. As late as 1851 only eighty stations in the provinces, including the chief cities and outposts, had been opened. Priority of service was secured to the government, and the Secretary of State was empowered, on extraordinary occasions, to take possession of all telegraph stations and hold them for a week, with power to continue so to do.

The tariff of charges adopted was, for twenty words, including address and signature, one penny per mile for the first fifty miles; one half-penny for the second fifty; and one farthing for any distance beyond 100 miles. The lowest charge was 2s. 6d., sterling. This tariff existed as late as 1851. Compare these rates with those of the American lines at the same period.

From London to York, a distance of about 230 miles, the charge was 9s., equal to $ 2.25 gold.

From New York to Boston, a distance of 220 miles, the tariff for ten words, exclusive of address and signature, was twenty cents!

From London to Edinburgh, a distance of about 400 miles, the charge was 13s., or $ 3.25, while from New York to Buffalo, 500 miles, the charge was forty cents. On the English tariff of charges, a message from New York to New Orleans would have been $ 11.46; the actual tariff was $ 2.50.

ACKNOWLEDGED SUPERIORITY OF THE EARLY AMERICAN SERVICE.

On this subject we have the testimony of one of the best of British popular publications, — "Chambers's Papers for the People," published in 1851, — whose words we quote : —

"The scale of charges in the United States is much lower than in this country ; the electric telegraph is consequently more available to the greater part of the population engaged in commercial affairs. Apart from business and politics, the Americans have made the telegraph subservient to other uses ; medical practitioners in distant towns have been consulted, and their prescriptions transmitted along the wire ; and a short time since a gallant gentleman in Boston married a lady in New York by telegraph, — a process which may supersede the necessity for elopement, provided the law hold the ceremony valid. A favorable idea of the immediate practical utility of the telegraph may be gathered from a communication to the present writer from New York. 'The telegraph,' he writes, 'is used in this country by all classes except the very poorest, the same as the mail. The most ordinary messages are sent in this way, — a joke, an invitation to a party, an inquiry about health, &c. At the offices they are accommodating, and will inquire about messages that have miscarried or have not been answered, without extra charge.' The lines in the United States are carried across the country regardless of travelled thoroughfares ; over tracts of sand and swamp, through the wild primeval forest where man has not yet begun his contest with nature, where even the rudiments of civilization are yet to be learned. Away it stretches, the metallic indicator of intellectual supremacy, traversing regions haunted by the rattlesnake and the alligator, solitudes that re-echo with nocturnal howlings of the wolf and the bear. Communications are maintained from North to South, East and West, through all the length and breadth of the mighty Union, and with a frequency and social purpose exceeding that of any other nation. In one stretch, Maine and Vermont, where winter with deepest snows and arctic temperature usurps six months of the year, are united with the lands of the tropics, where the magnolia blooms and palm-trees grow in perpetual summer. Subordinate lines bring the great lakes — the inland seas — into direct communication with the ocean ports on the eastern shore. Nothing stops the restless, enterprising spirit of that people."

REMARKABLY LOW TARIFFS OF THE EARLY AMERICAN TELEGRAPHS.

There is, indeed, nothing more remarkable respecting the presentation of any great invention to the public than the fact that the electric telegraph in America was thrown open to the public, in its very inception, at the lowest tariff which has yet, under all the excitement of opposition, been adopted.

What was true of Great Britain with respect to tariffs during the early years of the introduction of the telegraph applies, as has been seen, equally to France and the other European states. Every tariff adopted was, to a large extent, prohibitory, and the facts connected with these years utterly falsify the statement that Europe has shown (until within a very few years) anything like the spirit of liberality which private companies in the United States have manifested in this matter.

Since these early years no advance was made in our tariffs until the third year of the rebellion, when the depreciation of the currency necessitated the increasing of the salaries of employees from fifty to one hundred per cent, and enhanced the price of material in a corresponding ratio, compelling a considerable increase of the tariff on despatches. Since the war closed, most of the important tariffs have been reduced to their original standard, without any corresponding reduction of the price of material or labor.

In contrast with this, we need only to point to the large advance in railway fares and transportation, in the cost of entertainment at hotels, in the prices of daily newspapers, and in that of almost every commodity or service which the people enjoy; and yet the telegraph, like all other enterprises, has been burdened with the same increase in the cost of labor and materials.

NO SIMILARITY BETWEEN THE TELEGRAPH AND POSTAL SYSTEMS.

The idea which has been repeatedly broached, that the telegraph and postal communication are in the same category, is entirely fallacious. The telegraph does that which the post cannot do, and which, before the telegraph was invented, remained undone. If the public use the telegraph at a cost of 25 cents when they might use the mail at a cost of three cents, it is obvious that the use of the telegraph implies something essentially different from the use of the post. If they use the post, with its tardy departure and delivery, instead of the telegraph with its instant and continuous departure and delivery, it is equally obvious that there is something implied in the use of the post that is not to be obtained by the use of the telegraph.

Postal correspondence and telegraph communication are two very distinct things.

A telegram announces sudden illness; death; an accident; prices of gold every five minutes; prices of stocks every hour; sudden fluctuations in the values of commodities; orders rooms at a hotel, while the sender is *en route* and flying to the distant city as rapidly as steam can carry him; countermands orders and instructions contained in letters sent by post; orders letters to be returned unopened; orders the arrest of fugitives from justice after they have taken their departure on the railway; orders the search for a package left in the cars, and its return by a succeeding train; announces that the Merrimac has destroyed several ships of war, and may get to sea in spite of the Monitor and ravage the coast; announces that the flag has been fired upon at Charleston, and in twenty minutes arouses the entire nation. None of these things are possible for the post. Before a letter could convey the intelligence of the sudden illness, the patient is dead, or convalescent; the dead is buried; gold has changed in price a hundred times; stocks have gone up and down; the man arrives at his hotel twenty-four hours in advance of his letter; the instructions in the letters have been acted upon, and no subsequent ones can repair the damage; the fugitive from justice escapes out of the country; the package left in the cars is irretrievably lost; the Merrimac has been sent to the bottom, and the alarm caused by the tidings through the post, which must continue until another arrival, is groundless; and the flag has been insulted a month, before all the patriots of the country have heard the tidings by the slow, plodding mail.

The telegram is often the index to the more full and copious information conveyed by the post, but it does not supersede it. There is no similarity in the conveyance of matter by post or telegraph.

A letter deposited in a post-office is placed in a bag, and carried to its destination with no less labor and expense than if *ten* letters were so deposited. The time taken in transport is the same. A leather bag covers a thousand letters as easily as a solitary note. It was this fact which led to the reduction of postage. But it was accomplished without the loss of an hour to government, without the enlargement of a coach, or any considerable increase in the compensation paid for the service. It involved no new brain-labor, no new responsibilities, no new expense. Under such circumstances high postage was a folly, and to return to it would be almost a crime.

A communication by telegraph, on the contrary, demands a calm, unoccupied brain, and a steady hand to manipulate its contents, letter by letter. A slip of the finger from the manipulating key changes its meaning; a truant thought alters the manuscript; a shadow of forgetfulness mars its whole design. It demands a whole wire for its use, and a given time for its solitary passage. Hence the necessity for multiplying the wires and enlarging the operating staff.

Added to all this is the necessity for repeating this process when destined to any point not directly reached by the originating office.

Over and over again have many of the messages left in the hands of telegraph companies to be translated or re-written before they reach their destination; very different from the sealed letter, which needs but the toss of a practised hand to change its route and put it under the cover of a new bag.

The difference between the use of the post and telegraph is well shown by the practice of the Western Union Telegraph Company, *which requires all of its employees to use the mail, instead of the telegraph, in every case where the interests of the company will not suffer by the delay.* **All check** errors, and discrepancies in **ac**counts, are settled by correspondence through the mail, where **the** same might be **done** more readily, though at far greater expense, by the use of the wires. Now, if the company owning the lines, and working them, can better afford to pay the postage on its communications, than to block up the wires with its own free business, it shows a very radical difference between the expense of transmitting matter by steam, or horse-power, and doing the same by electricity.

COLLECTION AND DELIVERY **OF TELEGRAMS BY** LETTER-CARRIERS **IMPRACTICABLE.**

The plan proposed **for the collection and** delivery **of tele**grams by **letter-carriers is** equally impracticable. The rapid and safe **delivery** of messages is the great difficulty with which **the** telegraph companies have to contend, and the amount paid **for this service** forms a very material portion of the expense attending the operation of the **system. How** would this service be **performed** if left **to the Post-Office Department? In 1865 —** **the** last year containing the statistics **of** the number of **letters** sent through **the** United States mail — the Postmaster-General estimates the number of letters transmitted at 467,591,600. No statement of the total number of letters delivered by carrier in the United States is given in the Postmaster-General's reports for 1865 or 1866, but he states that the number of cities at which free delivery is established is 46, and the total number of carriers, 863; that 582 carriers **are** attached to ten offices, from which are delivered 38,060,009 letters. If **the** remaining 281 **carriers, who are** distributed among 36 offices, deliver as **many in proportion, we** have a total of **56,446,004 letters delivered** for **the year,** or about nine per cent **of the whole number** transmitted through the mail. This does not present a very flattering result, and does not argue very favorably for the satisfactory delivery of thirteen millions of **telegrams,** through the same channel, at over 4,000 offices!

Compare with these meagre results the operations of the British Post-Office, which employs 11,449 carriers, and annually delivers **705,000,000 letters.**

As for the collection of telegrams from street **boxes, the very**

idea is in direct antagonism to the first principles of telegraphic communication. A street box may answer the purpose of a place of deposit for a letter intended for the next day's mail, but those who desire to communicate by telegraph want immediate and speedy communication. They require their message conveyed, and very frequently answered, whilst they wait in the telegraph office. They have no idea of depositing their messages to await the diurnal collection from the street box. Indeed, the idea is too absurd to be seriously discussed. There are upwards of 100 telegraph offices in the city of New York alone, and a proportionate number of branch offices in all the cities. Is it probable that persons who wish to send a despatch will walk several miles to send it by government line rather than patronize private lines at their own doors ?

We cannot think that a department whose expenses exceed its receipts by $6,437,991.85 in a single year; which cannot even *guess within a hundred millions* of the number of letters it transmits per annum; which provides only forty-six free delivery offices out of a total of 29,387 post-offices in the United States; which does not even pretend to give the number of letters delivered free for any one year; and which sends over 4,500,000 letters to the Dead-Letter Office per annum, is a very proper guardian of so important an interest as the Electric Telegraph.

The space occupied for the various telegraph offices in all the principal cities of the United States is considerably greater than that required by the post-offices, while the rent paid by our company, owing to the more central and eligible situations of our offices, is greatly in excess of that paid by the Post-Office Department. In New York, our company pays $40,000 per annum for rent of its central office alone. So far as space and eligibility of location is concerned, we could much better accommodate the public by the delivery of their letters at our numerous offices, than they are now accommodated at the remote and inconvenient places provided for them by the government, and in all respects we could much better handle the mails than the post-office, as now located and generally conducted, could manage the telegraph.

MR. WASHBURNE'S PROPOSED EXPERIMENTAL LINE.

Mr. Washburne says : —

" In the present position of the finances of the country, it would hardly be wise to enter upon an extended experiment. It should be tried at first on a limited scale, and at small cost. If it proves successful, and becomes what the telegraph under other government control has become in other countries, — a source of revenue, as well as an inestimable boon to the community, — it ought to be, and doubtless will be, extended. The amount necessary to construct a suitable line from Washington to New York, and to sustain it until it becomes self-sustaining, will not exceed $75,000, and it is the belief of experienced telegraphers that, with a tariff of charges as low as that of Belgium and Switzerland, and with an additional charge of single postage upon each message, the line would be self-sustaining from the beginning, and would probably repay its entire cost long before the value of the structure was materially impaired."

The results of lowering tariffs for telegrams to a point approximating the charge for letter postage has been tried so often in this country, as not to require a new demonstration. The following statement will show the result of a recent trial between the two important cities of Chicago and Milwaukee.

On the 12th of August, 1867, a rival line was opened between those two points, having no connection with any other at either end. The competition, therefore, was for local business only. The tariff previously had been sixty cents. The average number of messages transmitted per day for the ten days preceding the beginning of business by the new company was sixty-nine, and the daily receipts fifty-five dollars. On the opening of the rival line the rate was reduced to forty cents, and the average number of messages sent by both was eighty-seven, the receipts forty-seven dollars. On the 16th September the rate was further reduced to twenty cents, with the following results : Average number of messages per day for both lines, one hundred and thirty-three. Average receipts, thirty-seven dollars. On November 8th the rate was reduced to ten cents, and remained so for the next fourteen days, during which the number of telegrams transmitted daily by both lines was one hundred and sixty-seven, and the average receipts twenty-six dollars.

About the 20th November the rates were advanced to forty cents, by mutual agreement, and afterwards the lines and records of the new company came into our possession.

No. 1.

Statement showing number of Messages sent between Chicago and Milwaukee for first twelve days in August, 1867, at a Tariff of sixty cents, and same for 1868, at a Tariff of forty cents, together with daily Receipts.

DATE.		August, 1867. Tariff 60 and 4.			August, 1868. Tariff 40 and 3.		
		Sent.	Received.	Receipts.	Sent.	Received.	Receipts.
August	1	41	48	$ 67.40	49	37	$ 39.64
"	2	31	38	57.00	4	2	1.87
"	3	36	25	49.63	53	42	58.25
"	4	2	1	1.78	69	39	53.02
"	5	41	34	55.98	46	41	43.36
"	6	41	40	63.39	67	46	54.60
"	7	42	49	73.77	51	39	42.44
"	8	45	27	55.75	56	50	52.08
"	9	39	38	61.68			
"	10	40	40	63.91	52	44	47.30
"	11				62	42	51.70
Totals . . .		358	340	$ 550.29	°509	382	$ 444.26

1867, Average, 69 Messages . . . . $ 55.00
1868, " 89 " 44.42

No. 2.

Statement showing the number of Messages transmitted between Chicago and Milwaukee, over the Western Union and Independent Telegraph Lines, from August 12th to August 26th, together with the daily Receipts.

DATE		Tariff 40 and 3.					
		W. U. and Independent. August, 1867.			Western Union. August, 1868.		
		Sent.	Received.	Receipts.	Sent.	Received.	Receipts.
August	12	33	47	$ 52.96	44	42	$ 47.82
"	13	35	52	66.35	49	38	50.11
"	14	35	50	59.00	54	42	53.35
"	15	44	46	55.27	52	41	48.28
"	16	34	45	53.61	1		.52
"	17	38	45	62.38	58	52	63.21
"	18		2	2.02	45	33	45.69
"	19	45	51	70.45	40	45	52.39
"	20	41	50	68.51	47	44	64.77
"	21	39	46	62.67	54	40	50.22
"	22	37	39	49.42	48	38	46.77
"	23	39	41	52.97	3	2	2.21
"	24	30	33	56.15	43	45	59.57
"	25	2		2.10	54	66	73.26
"	26	63	41	55.31	48	57	62.89
Totals		515	588	$ 769.17	640	585	$ 721.06

1867, Average, 73 Messages . . . . $ 51.28
1868, " 81 " 48.07

Statement **No. 1 exhibits a** comparison for **the first** ten days of August, 1867, before the opening of the rival line, and when the tariff was sixty **cents, with** the same period in 1868 after the tariff **had been** forty **cents for nearly a year.** Statement No. 2 makes **a** similar comparison between the aggregate business of the Western Union and the competing line for the first fifteen days after the latter opened in 1867, and the same period in 1868, when, although **the** rate was the same, there was no competition. **By** Table No. 1 **it** appears that, at a tariff of sixty **cents,** the number of messages **per** day last year was sixty-nine, **and the** receipts **therefor** fifty-**five** dollars. That during the same **period this year, at a** reduction of one third in the tariff, **there was an increase of about** thirty-three and **one third per cent in the number** of messages, but a loss in revenue **of** twenty per cent. In other words, our work has been considerably increased, and **our** compensation therefor sensibly **diminished.** Statement No. 2 shows that last year, under **the stimulus of active** competition, and a reduction in rates of **one third, the** average number of messages **per day for** fifteen **days was** but four more than for the **ten** days **next** preceding. **It also** shows that, after the reduced **rate had** been in operation **a year,** and, notwithstanding the fact that the telegraph business in all sections of the country in the month of August this year was somewhat larger than last, the average had been increased but eight messages per day, and this increase was attended by a loss of over three dollars per day in the revenue.

From September 1 **to** November **3,** 1868, the number of messages **transmitted per day between these** places **was one** hundred four **and a quarter, and the average** daily receipts $ 56.41.

On the 4th **of November** another rival **line was opened** between Chicago **and** Milwaukee, but no change **in rates was** introduced until the 24th of November. The average number of messages transmitted per **day by** the Western Union Telegraph **Company** between these **places,** from the 4th to the 23d **of November,** inclusive, **was** seventy-eight, and the daily receipts $ 43.27.

On the 24th of November the rates were reduced to twenty **cents per message,** with the following results : Average number of messages transmitted per day between Chicago and Milwaukee by the Western Union Telegraph Company, sixty-eight; average daily receipts, $ 24.59.

It should be remembered that the business from which these exhibits are derived is between two of the most important inland commercial cities in the country. Both are largely interested in two important branches of commerce, — grain and lumber ; and probably no other points could be selected from which more reliable results could be obtained.

The reason why the Chicago and Milwaukee table is the only one given to show the results of competition is, that such comparisons are only valuable when they exhibit the effect upon the business of both competitors. This is impossible in other cases, because our opponents will not furnish us with their figures. We have written to every Telegraph Company in the United States for such statistics for publication, but none of them has responded to our request.

LONDON DISTRICT TELEGRAPH COMPANY.

We copy the following official statement of the London District Telegraph Company from the Telegraphic Journal, London, July 30, 1864. The capital of the company is £ 60,000, and the average cost of telegrams transmitted over its lines, for distances that cannot exceed ten miles, was 6d., equal to eighteen cents in our currency, and yet the loss in four and a half years' business was £ 9,573 3s. 7d. : —

Statement showing the Receipts and Expenditures of the London District Telegraph Company from December, 1859, to June, 1864.

Half-year ending	Number of Messages.	Receipts for Messages.			Expenditures.			Deficiency.		
		£	s.	d.	£	s.	d.	£	s.	d.
June, 1860	26,155	550	19	11	2,282	10	7	4,326	2	4
December, 1860	47,365	1,058	19	2	3,294	0	6	2,168	1	7
June, 1861	64,785	2,137	1	7	4,394	12	3	2,177	11	4
December, 1861	77,939	2,592	15	10	4,663	5	4	1,995	13	7
June, 1862	123,280	3,956	4	8	5,077	17	11	1,077	15	4
December, 1862	124,222	3,999	3	2	4,958	4	2	894	0	4
June, 1863	129,710	4,216	6	11	4,721	1	3	440	9	4
December, 1863	131,216	4,326	4	0	5,125	9	4	796	15	4
June, 1864	152,795	4,802	10	0	4,863	17	10	60	12	0

The Directors of the **above company** express much satisfaction in being able to present to the shareholders so favorable a statement of its business; but it strikes us that a system which entailed a **net** loss of one sixth of the capital invested in a little **over four** years is not a desirable one for imitation.

TELEGRAPHS UNDER GOVERNMENT AND PRIVATE CONTROL COMPARED.

The assertion that the Telegraph facilities are better in those countries where it is under governmental control **than in those** where it is left to private enterprise **is** entirely erroneous, as the following tables, compiled from **official data, will show.**

Statistics of Telegraphs constructed and operated **under Government** *Control.*

NAME OF COUNTRY.	Number of Offices.	Number of Miles of Line.	Number of Miles of Wire.	Number of Messages Sent.	Population.	Proportion of Offices to Population.
Austria . . .	851	24,618	73,854	2,507,472	39,411,309	1 to 46,311
Belgium . . .	356	2,187	6,146	1,128,005	4,984,451	1 to 14,000
Bavaria . . .		2,115	4,945		4,541,556	
Denmark. . .	89		2,515	308,150	2,468,713	1 to 27,000
France . . .	1,209	20,628	68,687	2,507,472	38,302,625	1 to 31,600
Italy . . .	529	8,200	20,120	1,760,889	25,925,717	1 to 49,000
Norway . . .	73			269,375	1,433,488	1 to 19,000
Prussia . . .	538	18,386	55,149	1,964,003	17,739,913	1 to 33,000
Russia . . .	308	12,013	22,214	838.653	68,224,832	1 to 221,000
Switzerland . .	252	1,858	3,717	668,916	2,510,494	1 to 10,000
Spain	142	8,871	17,743	533,376	16,302,625	1 to 109,000
	4,347	98,876	275,090	12,486,311		

Statistics of Telegraphs **constructed and operated under Private Control.**

NAME OF COUNTRY.	Number of Offices.	Number of Miles of Line.	Number of Miles of Wire.	Number of Messages Sent.	Population.	Proportion of Offices to Population.
Great Britain and Ireland . .	2,151	16,588	80,466	5,781,189	29,591,009	1 to 13,714
Dominion of Canada	382	6,747	8,935	573,219	3,976,224	1 to 10,400
United States .	4,126	62,782	125,564	12,386,952	31,148,047	1 to 7,549
	6,659	86,117	214,965	18,741,360		

Thus it will be seen **that Continental Europe,** where the telegraphs are under government control, furnishes but **4,347 offices** for a population of over 250,000,000, while Great Britain, the Dominion of Canada, and the United States, where telegraphy has been left to the control of the people, untrammelled by governmental interference, monopoly, or restriction, furnish 6,659 offices for a population of 64,000,000 ! The number of telegrams transmitted per annum in Continental Europe is only 12,486,311, while there were sent by the people of the three countries where it has hitherto been free from government repression, 18,741,360. The tariff of charges in Continental Europe averages eighty-one cents per message, while in the three countries where the people manage the business it averages but fifty-one cents.

Private enterprise alone laid the submarine cables through the Persian Gulf and Mediterranean Sea, across the Gulf of St. Lawrence, the Vineyard Sound, the Strait of Florida, the English Channel, the North Sea, and the German and Atlantic Oceans.

THE TELEGRAPH AND THE PRESS.

In nothing, perhaps, is the superiority of private enterprise over governmental control more strongly marked than in the extraordinary amount of news furnished to the press of the United States, as contrasted by the meagre supply of the European journals.

By a system of co-operation among the newspapers of the United States and the Western Union Telegraph Company, the news of the world is daily furnished to the people of every portion of this country at a price within the reach of the poorest citizen.

On page 8 we have shown that 294,503,630 words are annually furnished to the newspapers of the United States, at an average cost of less than two mills per word. This immense amount of matter is not transmitted to each newspaper separately, but through a combination of wires only possible to a vast system like that owned by the Western Union Telegraph Company, it is sent to a large number of places simultaneously, with only one transmission.

The newspapers of the United States are associated together on the co-operative system. There is a general association having its headquarters in New York, which collects news from every part of the world ; and there are local associations in every section of the country, which furnish their quota of intelligence to the general association, and receive in return such news as they require.

As an illustration of the manner in which this service is performed, we will take the State press of New York for an example. The report is compiled by the agent of the Association for the various editions of the newspapers requiring it, and it is then handed to the telegrapher, who with the manipulation of his magic key transmits it simultaneously to Poughkeepsie, Hudson, Albany, Troy, Utica, Syracuse, Auburn, Elmira, Binghamton, Owego, Rome, Oswego, Rochester, and Buffalo, New York, to Rutland and Burlington, Vermont, and to Scranton, Pennsylvania. These stations are not all on a single wire, nor on the same route, and the question may be asked, How can they all receive the same information from a single impulse ? This is accomplished by a combination of circuits through an instrument called a repeater, by which the intelligence can be transmitted to a thousand offices as easily as to one.

The news is sent to the Eastern press in a similar manner. The manipulation of the key at New York transmits the report simultaneously to Bridgeport, New Haven, Hartford, Waterbury, and Norwich, Conn., Providence, R. I., and to Springfield, Worcester, Boston, Fall River and New Bedford, Mass.

The operator at each of these places receives the reports by the click of the instruments, — reading by the sound of the armature, — and with an agate pen copies them upon manifold paper, making as many impressions as are necessary to furnish each paper with a duplicate copy.

Direct wires carry and bring news from and to Chicago, Cincinnati, St. Louis, Washington, New Orleans, Plaister Cove, and other important points. Sixteen wires work out of New York every night to transmit or receive news reports, and all over the United States the ubiquitous iron threads are permeated by the subtile and invisible fluid during all the silent hours of the night, conveying intelligence of passing events in all sections of the civilized world for publication in the morning journals throughout the country.

It is a singular and suggestive fact, that the amount of news which we furnish to the press of the United States, for an aggregate sum of $521,509, is considerably greater than the entire telegraphic correspondence of Continental Europe, for which the paternal governments of those enlightened and enterprising peoples receive $11,597,632.71.

The following table will serve to show the remarkable contrast, in this respect, between the systems under government and private control. The number of messages delivered to the press are obtained for this comparison by dividing the total number of words furnished to the press by 20, the European standard: —

Statement showing the Average Cost of Telegrams in Continental Europe and the Average Cost of Press Telegrams in the United States, with Total Amount of each per annum.

Total number of messages transmitted in Continental Europe for the year 1866, 12,902,538 Gross receipts for the above,............ $11,597,632.71	Total number of messages furnished to the newspapers of the United States for 1866,............... 14,725,181 Gross receipts for the above,. $521,509
Average cost of telegrams in Continental Europe,............ 81 cts.	Average cost of press telegrams in the United States,........ 3½ cts.

The above exhibit illustrates the difference between what can be accomplished under a popular government which leaves the press and telegraph free and untrammelled, and the results of the paternal system which the governments of Continental Europe impose upon their subjects. For these great benefits the people of this country are indebted to the government for the one negative quality of letting the press and telegraph alone. For the positive quality which actually provides them they are solely indebted to the enterprise and public spirit of the press, and the Western Union Telegraph Company, the latter furnishing the reports at a price which barely covers the cost of service employed in transmitting them, and leaving nothing to defray the expense of the wear of the lines, or interest on the investments for their construction.

In no other country in the world is there such a system, and in none can there ever be, until the policy of our government is imitated, and the people left to manage their own private affairs, leaving the press and the telegraph free and untrammelled by governmental **control or** repression. What our government, with such **an** example **already** set, might be able or disposed to do, in the event of **its monopolizing the** telegraphs, it is impossible to say ; but it is unquestionably true, that no other government has ever made such **a** use of them to promote the education and general well-being of its people.

We believe **it** would prove a serious misfortune to the press and **the people, if the** government were to destroy, by **its** interference, this admirable co-operative system of obtaining telegraphic **news at** such low rates.

The tariff for special press **reports is as** follows : **For** the first one hundred words, **full** rates ; **for the next four** hundred words, a discount **of thirty-three and one** third per **cent ; for** the **next** five hundred words, one half the ordinary tariff ; and all over **one** thousand **words, a** discount is made of sixty-six and two thirds per **cent.**

Mr. Washburne's bill provides for **a** general tariff of one cent **per** word for telegrams, with **an** additional charge of three cents **for** postage, **and two cents for delivery, and stipulates that a re-**duction of not **more than fifty per cent shall be made for press** reports. *This* **rate** *would increase* **the average** *cost* **of news for** *the press of the United States more than* **three** *hundred* **per** *cent, and thus* **the** *newspapers would* **be** *compelled to pay an extra tax of a* **million dollars per** *annum for the privileges they now enjoy.*

If these facts show any results to warrant governmental assump-tion **or interference in the business of** telegraphing, we fail to per-ceive **them.**

REVIEW

MR. GARDINER G. HUBBARD'S LETTER TO THE POSTMASTER-GENERAL ON THE EUROPEAN AND AMERICAN SYSTEMS OF TELEGRAPH.

WE have recently received a pamphlet from Gardiner G. Hubbard, Esq., of Boston, entitled a "Letter to the Postmaster-General on the European and American Systems of Telegraph, with Remedy for the present High Rates," which we will briefly review.

Mr. Hubbard commences by saying: —

"The reasons that have induced the public to commit to the government the transmission of the mails by rail have induced most civilized nations to intrust it with the duty of transmitting correspondence by telegraph. England and America are the only important exceptions."

As England and America are the only "civilized nations" where the public have any control of such matters, there need be no further discussion of this proposition.

ERRONEOUS STATEMENTS RELATIVE TO BELGIAN TELEGRAPHS.

Alluding to the Belgian telegraph, Mr. Hubbard says : —

"In 1850 the private lines then in operation were purchased by the government, and have since been under its management. The rates were originally one franc and a half for a message of twenty words. At these rates, the telegraph was little used for inland messages, and its development was very slow. In January, 1863, they were reduced to one franc, and December, 1865, to half a franc."

By referring to the official tables published by the Belgian government, on page 94, it will be seen that the average cost per message on the Belgian lines in 1851 and 1852 was over 6 francs ; in 1853, 5.10 francs ; 1854 and 1855, over 4 francs ; in 1856 and 1857, 3.62 and 3.42 francs ; from 1858 to 1862, over 2 francs ; and even in 1867 they averaged 0.85 francs.

We quote from Mr. Hubbard again : —

"In 1862, the inland messages, at 1½ francs, numbered 105,274
" 1865, " " " at 1 franc, " 332,718
" 1867, " " " at ½ franc, " 819,668

Total receipts in 1866, ... 961,112 francs.
" expenses in " . . . . . 839,000 "

Estimated profits for 1866 on the entire business, if no reduction had been made, ... 198,499 "
Actual profits for 1866, under the reduced rates, . 122,112 "

Actual loss by reducing the rates on inland messages one half, ... 76,387 "

By an examination of Table H, page 96, it will be seen that the total receipts of the Belgian telegraphs for 1866 were 962,213 francs ; expenditures, 1,217,496 francs ; loss, 255,283 francs. Of the receipts only 407,532 francs were for inland messages, of which there were transmitted 692,536, while 553,580 francs were received for 435,469 international and transit messages. As before stated, the expense of service upon transit messages is merely nominal. They simply pass through the kingdom, and require no labor in receiving, transmitting, or delivery. The greater part of the expense, therefore, was incurred upon the inland messages ; and, had not the Belgian administration imposed a tax upon neighboring nations of 553,580 francs for messages coming from or going to other countries, there would have been a deficit of 809,964 francs on the year's business instead of 255,283 francs.

We quote from Mr. Hubbard : —

" A system of railroads is also owned and operated by the government, and the telegraph is connected with both the railroad and the post. A large proportion of the offices are at the railway stations, but every post-office is an office of deposit, from which messages are despatched at once, free of charge, to the nearest telegraph office, when in the same district ; otherwise, by the first messenger or by special carrier, on payment of an extra rate for porterage. This union of the telegraph with the post and railroad reduces the expenses for operators, clerks, general management, rent and office expenses, and brings the system into close connection with every citizen.

"The rates are prepaid by stamps, and are uniform and low. The rate for all inland messages by telegraph, or by telegraph and post where the place of deposit or delivery is not on the line of the telegraph, is one half franc [or thirteen and a half cents currency]."

BELGIAN TELEGRAMS DELIVERED BY POST.

In reply to this flattering picture of the Belgian system of telegraphy we quote the following from a recent English publication : * —

"The government of Belgium not only have a monopoly of the telegraphs and post-office, but also of most of the railways of the country. They work the system as a whole. In the case of ordinary half-franc telegrams, the messages are not uniformly despatched by messenger from the office at which they arrive, *but are sent to the residence of the receiver by post!*

"The administration of the Belgian telegraph in no respect holds itself responsible for the delivery of a message, unless it is specially insured and additionally paid for. They decline all responsibility on account of delay in the transmission or non-arrival of a half-franc telegram. *They will not even inquire into the cause of delay of a half-franc telegram!* No matter how long a message has taken in delivery, or whatever may be the errors in it, the government will make no compensation to the sender or receiver, except under very exceptional circumstances. Moreover, the twenty words forwarded for half a franc includes addresses both of sender and receiver, ' all of which is free in this country.'"

For further particulars relative to the Belgian telegraph service reference is made to pages 5, 7, 8, 13, 16 – 24.

WANT OF UNIFORMITY IN RATES.

We quote from Mr. Hubbard : —

"There is no uniformity in the rates. They are often less to a distant station than to an intermediate one on the same line. An

---

* Government and the Telegraphs. London, 1868.

estimate of the average rates, and of the annual number of messages transmitted has been made by ascertaining the rates to seventy-one stations at different distances from Boston, and arranging them in four different classes."

Mr. Hubbard groups his American distances into classes of 500, 1,000, 1,500, and 2,000 miles; while his English classes embrace those of 100 and under, 200 and under; over 200, and to Ireland.

The average rates he gives for America for

Class A,	500 miles and under,	.	.	.	$0.41
" B, over 500, and under 1,000,		.	.	.	1.43
" C, " 1,000, " " 1,500,		.	.	.	2.46
" D, " 1,500, " " 2,000,		.	.	.	3.36

The English rate for

Class A, less than 100 miles, one shilling, equal to $0.33 U. S. currency.

" B, between 100 and 200 miles, one			
shilling and sixpence,	"	0.50	"
" C, over 200 miles, two shillings,	"	0.66	"
" D, to Ireland, three to four "	"	1.00 to 1.33	"

Mr. Hubbard says : —

" As rates are higher in America, a greater proportion of messages are sent to stations in class A than in England, and a smaller proportion to class D. The average receipt per message, at these rates, is $1.00. The gross receipts of the Western Union Company, for the year ending the 30th of June, 1868, were $6,952,273.* This sum, divided by the average receipts, gives the whole number of messages transmitted, viz. 6,952,000.

" It may be objected that those estimates are incorrect, and therefore the deductions are unreliable. If the Western Union Telegraph Company furnish a statement of messages annually transmitted, the required corrections will be made. If it is not given, it will be because the estimates of the average rates are too low, and the deductions too favorable to that company." †

As the average of these English rates is a little over 75 cents,

* This amount embraces the total revenue of the Western Union Telegraph Company for that year, and includes the receipts for telegrams, press reports, and from all other sources.

† The statement on page 7, of the number of messages annually transmitted by this company, shows that Mr. Hubbard's estimate gives less than 70 per cent of the number actually sent over the wires. The average rate per message in the United States is fifty-seven cents.

while the greatest distance for the highest English class is less than for the shortest American class, which he averages at 41 cents, we do not see how he can assert that the American rates are higher than the English!

In answer to the charge of want of uniformity in the tariffs, we would call attention to the fact, that the lines under our control were constructed by a great number of separate organizations, having tariffs upon all bases, which had to be added together at all the termini of two or more lines, so that a message going a few hundred miles would require the payment sometimes of two or three rates. For instance, a few years since there were five telegraph companies owning the lines connecting Portland, Maine, with Cleveland, Ohio, and the tariff between these two places was ascertained by the addition of the local rates from Portland to Boston, Boston to Springfield, Springfield to Albany, Albany to Buffalo, and from Buffalo to Cleveland. The same system prevailed throughout the United States, until after the consolidation of the lines made it possible to transmit messages between places thousands of miles apart without the necessity of booking or rechecking at intermediate points. This result necessitated a remodelling of the tariffs, and the work has been going on uninterruptedly ever since; but when it is considered that a complete revision of the system required a separate tariff-sheet to be made out for over three thousand offices, changing and equalizing the rates to more than three thousand other offices, the immense labor and responsibility incurred in the undertaking may be imagined. It was impossible to effect this revision at once with any number of clerks, and for obvious reasons only a limited number could be employed upon it, as they can only act under the instruction of the executive officers, who are charged with all the other duties of an extensive organization.

Various plans have been suggested for simplifying and equalizing the tariffs, but difficulties of a practical nature present themselves in all of them. The existence of rival lines, built by speculators whose profit is in the construction of them, and which essay to do business at rates less than the cost of the service, necessitates the reduction of our rates along certain routes disproportionately, and prevents the adoption of a general rate strictly proportioned to distance. In the course of the coming year, however, it is expected that the work of revising our whole tariff system will be accomplished, to the satisfaction of all.

ASSERTION THAT COMMERCIAL MESSAGES ARE TRANSMITTED AT A LOSS.

Mr. Hubbard's assertion that the lowest rate between any large cities in America is 25 cents is incorrect. The tariff between Washington and Baltimore is 10 cents ; between New York and Providence, New Haven, Hartford, &c., 20 cents.

If it is true, as he states, that " at these rates, under the present system, commercial messages are probably transmitted at a loss," it may be a matter of regret to the stockholders of the telegraph companies, but affords no just ground for governmental interference. Besides, how will his proposed corporation be able to make money by doing the business at a still lower rate ?

Mr. Hubbard says : —

" The history of the telegraph will explain the causes of these different rates. Great competition, in 1852, caused a large reduction in the rates. Soon after the validity of Mr. Morse's patent was confirmed by the courts many of the competing companies were enjoined and compelled to wind up or sell out, and some failed. In the Eastern and Southern States the American Telegraph Company, in which Mr. Morse and his friends were largely interested, bought out most of the old companies, and continued to occupy their territory for many years without serious opposition.

" The various companies in the West, South, and Northwest (forming groups of feeble organization) were gradually merged into one corporation, under the name of the Western Union Telegraph Company. In 1864, the United States Telegraph Company was organized to oppose this monopoly, and entered into a vigorous competition with the Western Union ; prices were reduced in consequence, and the business increased with great rapidity. In 1866 the American Telegraph Company, the United States Telegraph Company, and the Western Union were united under the corporate name of the last corporation ; the prices were again raised, and this first caused a less ratio of increase, and finally an actual decrease in the telegraphic business of the country."

Mr. Hubbard's pamphlet contains a statement of the rates between New York and Boston in former years which is inaccurate. The following is a correct table of the rates between those cities for the years 1849–52.

> In 1849 the rate was 30 cents.
> " 1850 " " " 20 "
> " 1851 " " " 20 "
> " 1852 " " " 10 "

CORRECTION OF ERRONEOUS STATEMENTS.]

The statement that " soon after the validity of the Morse patent was confirmed by the courts in 1852 many of the competing companies were enjoined and compelled to wind up or sell out " is incorrect, as is also the assertion that " the American Telegraph Company bought out most of the old companies, and continued to occupy their territory for many years without serious opposition."

The validity of the Morse patent was never disputed. In 1849 the Morse patentees commenced suits against the New York and New England [Bain] Telegraph Company, and the New York and Boston [House printing] Telegraph Company, for an infringement of the Morse patent. The case against the company using the Bain patent never came to trial, while the other was decided in favor of the defendant, by Judge Woodbury of the United States Supreme Court, 1850.*

The consolidations between competing lines, in 1852 and 1853, was caused by the inability of the companies under separate organizations to meet their working expenses. They were generally confined, however, to the union of the Morse and Bain lines, and there still remained two competing lines upon all the principal routes. There has never been but a single year, since 1849, when there have not been at least two competing lines between Boston and Washington.

The American Telegraph Company was not organized until 1855, and it was not consolidated with any opposition line until 1860. The next year after the consolidation the Independent

---

* For an abstract of this decision see " Prescott's History, Theory, and Practice of the Electric Telegraph." Boston : Fields, Osgood, & Co.

♦

Company built a competing line between New York and Portland, Maine.

The assertion that " the United States Telegraph Company was organized to oppose this monopoly, and entered into a vigorous competition with the Western Union, and that prices were reduced in consequence," is also incorrect. The United States Telegraph Company never reduced the rates at any point. On the contrary, it was not until after the United States' lines were put in operation that the rates were advanced. This was rendered necessary by the great depreciation of our currency, and consequent advance in the cost of labor and materials for working the lines, and was done by agreement of all the companies.

TARIFFS NOT INCREASED BY CONSOLIDATION OF THE LINES.

The statement that, after the consolidation of the American, United States, and Western Union Telegraph Companies, in 1866, " the prices were again raised, and this first caused a less ratio of increase, and finally an actual decrease in the telegraphic business of the country," is without the least foundation in fact. In no instance has the tariff been increased since the consolidation. On the contrary, there has been a steady decrease, the rates to more than one thousand stations having been lowered since the consolidation ; and this course is still being pursued as rapidly as a just regard to the rights of the stockholders and the extremely complicated nature of adjustment to be made will allow.

The impression which Mr. Hubbard attempts to give, that the consolidation of the companies forming the Western Union Telegraph Company, included all the lines, and gave this company a monopoly of the business, is also incorrect. The Franklin Company, between Boston and New York, the Insulated Company, between Boston and Washington, the Bankers and Brokers', between New York and Washington, and others, were then in active operation, and are still.

Mr. Hubbard says : —

" In other countries, the rates are reduced with the growth of business, and are never raised. In this country, they are reduced by competition, followed by consolidation of the competing companies, and subsequent increase of rates, without regard to the growth of the business."

The rates are unquestionably often reduced by competition, sometimes below the cost of doing the business, and this will always be the case as long as men will listen to the plausible schemes of speculative enthusiasts, and invest their money in new lines in the hope of realizing profits which are never earned. The assertion, however, that consolidation is followed by an increase of rates, without regard to the growth of the business, is not warranted by the facts.

ERRONEOUS ASSERTION THAT A LARGE PROPORTION OF THE OFFICES ARE AT RAILROAD STATIONS.

We quote from Mr. Hubbard again : —

" The telegraph in this country is very generally connected with the railroad system, and a large proportion of the offices are at railroad stations.* These are seldom in the centre of the towns, and are not resorted to as generally as the post-office. In the large cities, the principal offices are near the business centres, with a number of secondary offices, generally at hotels and railroad stations. The rent of the main offices is very large, and the expenses for operators, clerks, and managers are also necessarily much more than when the telegraph is connected with the post."

It is true that many telegraph offices are connected with the railroad system in this country, as well as abroad. Indeed, no railroad would be considered complete without such a connection, but it is not true that a large proportion of the offices are at the railroad stations.

We have shown on page 8 that the telegraph system of Europe is not specially connected with the Post-Office Department. In some countries the telegraph, post-office, and railway systems are under one department, but there is no particular connection between them. The post-offices are merely offices of deposit for telegrams, and not for transmission. But supposing they were united, why should the expenses of operators, clerks, and managers

* By a singular coincidence, Mr. Scudamore makes the same complaint against the English companies, and in nearly the same words. See Scudamore's Letter to the Postmaster-General, London, 1863.

be necessarily **much less than when the** telegraph is worked separately? **We presume he does not** propose to dispense with the operators, and put the **telegrams in the** mail-bag; or does he propose that when the government gets control of the telegraph that the salaries will be reduced? If **this is** his idea, we think he is reckoning on **a** false hope, for if there was an attempt of this nature, the operators would seek some other employment.

AMERICAN **AND** EUROPEAN TELEGRAPH TARIFFS **COMPARED.**

Mr. Hubbard says : —

" The lowest **American** rates **are** higher than the average foreign rates, and **the** average **rates** several times higher than the foreign. These high rates **retard** the development of the system, which was more rapid in its early growth in this than in any other country. What are the reasons assigned for these high rates? Are they well founded, and if not, how can they be obviated? "

These assertions **are** entirely erroneous, **and the facts** quite the **reverse.** *The highest American* **rates are lower than the** *highest foreign rates ; the average American rates are lower* **than** *the average foreign rates ;* **and the lowest American** *rates are* **lower** *than the lowest foreign rates.* The lowest **rate given** in Europe **is** half **a franc,** about equal to 14⅖ cents in currency, while our **rate between** Baltimore and Washington is only 10 cents. In Paris the tariff on city messages is half a franc (14⅖ cents), and in London, for city messages, 6*d.* sterling, equal to 18 cents in our currency; while the rates for **New York, from the** Battery to Harlem River, are only **10 cents.**

In order **that a fair** comparison **may be made between the** American and **European** systems of telegraphy, so far as the rate of charges is concerned, we present a list of sixty **of** the principal stations in Europe, and **the** same number in **the** United States, **with** the tariffs and **distances in air** lines from London and New **York respectively, together** with the rules and regulations of each system.

RULES OF THE EUROPEAN TELEGRAPHS.

The minimum charge is for a message of twenty words, including the address and signature, and half price is charged for each ten or fraction of ten words above twenty.

Words of seven or less syllables count as one word. In words containing more than seven, the overplus counts as *one* word; each word *underlined* counts as *three* words.

Messages containing the same subject-matter addressed to different stations are charged as separate messages.

Secret or cipher messages can be sent by government only.

Replies at full rates can be prepaid; but should the reply contain more than the number of words specified and paid for, the sender of the reply must pay for the excess as a fresh message.

Messages can be repeated by payment of double charge at the time they are sent, the words "Repetition paid" being inserted after receiver's address, and charged for.

All complaints respecting irregularity in the transmission or delivery of messages must be made by THE SENDER, and in cases of delay or error the complaint must invariably be accompanied by the RECEIVER'S COPY of the message. Complaints from the receivers of messages will not be entertained.

RULES OF THE WESTERN UNION TELEGRAPH COMPANY.

The minimum tariff is for a message of ten words. No charge is made for address, signature, or date. After the first ten words the rate is so much per word, the amount being proportional to the rate for the first ten.

All words are counted as one which are found so written in the dictionaries. No extra charge is made for messages written in cipher, and no restrictions are placed upon their transmission.

Replies can be prepaid if desired, and no charge is made for inserting this information in the sender's message.

Messages can be repeated by the payment of one half the regular charge in addition, and the company agrees to be responsible for any mistakes which may occur in repeated messages, to the amount of fifty times the sum received for sending the same.

Correctness in the transmission of messages to any point on the lines of this company can be INSURED by contract in writing, stating agreed amount of risk, and payment of premium thereon at the following rates, in addition to the usual charge for repeated messages, viz.: one per cent for any distance not exceeding one thousand miles, and two per cent for any greater distance. No employee of the company is authorized to vary the foregoing.

Statement showing the Minimum Rate for Telegrams from London to Principal Cities in Europe, and from New York to Principal Cities in America.

From London	Distance in Eng. Miles.	Tariff.			From New York	Distance in Eng. Miles.	Tariff.
		£	s. d.	U. S. Cur.			$ cts.
To Cambridge	40	1	6	=$0.52	To New Haven, Conn.	70	0.20
Dover	50	2	0	= 0.70	Hartford, Conn.	100	0.20
Birmingham	100	1	0	= 0.35	Providence, R. I.	150	0.20
Worcester	100	2	0	= 0.70	Springfield, Mass.	125	0.30
Havre	125	3	6	= 1.22	Worcester, "	155	0.30
Liverpool	180	1	0	= 0.35	Boston, "	190	0.30
Caen	160	5	0	= 1.75	Portsmouth, N. H.	200	0.45

From London	Distance in Eng. Miles.	£	s.	d.	U.S. Cur.	From New York	Distance in Eng. Miles.	$ cts.
To Plymouth	190		2	6	= 0.87	To Washington, D. C.	190	0.40
Paris	200		5	0	= 1.75	Augusta, Me.	280	0.65
Amsterdam	200		6	6	= 2.27	Oswego, N. Y.	250	0.40
Rheims	250		5	0	= 1.75	Portland, Me.	250	0.65
Aix-la-Chapelle	265		5	0	= 1.75	Bath, "	275	0.65
Wakefield	300		5	0	= 1.75	Rochester, N. Y.	280	0.50
Dublin	290		5	0	= 1.75	Pittsburg, Pa.	300	0.45
Edinburgh	320		4	0	= 1.40	Camden, Me.	330	0.65
Rochelle	350		7	3	= 2.53	Belfast, "	350	0.65
Frankfort	380		7	6	= 2.62	Buffalo, N. Y.	330	0.50
Hamburg	380		8	0	= 2.80	Erie, Pa.	360	1.00
Strasburg	385		7	3	= 2.53	Bangor, Me.	340	0.65
Hanover	400		8	0	= 2.80	Cleveland, Ohio	425	1.00
Stuttgart	420		7	6	= 2.62	Toledo, "	470	1.00
Berne	450		7	3	= 2.53	Columbus, "	475	0.95
Bordeaux	455		7	3	= 2.53	Sandusky, "	480	1.40
Munich	540		8	6	= 2.67	Cincinnati, "	550	1.00
Turin	550		7	3	= 3.53	Lexington, Ky.	575	1.00
Copenhagen	552		8	0	= 2.80	Dayton, Ohio	552	1.00
Berlin	560		10	0	= 3.50	Charleston, S. C.	590	2.00
Milan	575		8	6	= 2.67	Fort Wayne, Ind.	580	1.70
Marseilles	576		8	6	= 2.67	Lansing, Mich.	590	1.85
Prague	600		9	9	= 3.41	Louisville, Ky.	625	1.00
Modena	650		9	6	= 3.32	Indianapolis, Ind.	650	1.90
Saragossa	652		9	6	= 3.32	New Albany, "	660	1.75
Christiania	700		17	6	= 5.95	La Fayette, Ind.	700	1.95
Trieste	720		11		= 3.85	Chicago, Ill.	730	1.75
Vienna	780		11		= 3.85	Racine, Wis.	750	1.90
Madrid	750		10	6	= 3.67	Milwaukee, Wis.	770	1.90
Ancona	800		11		= 3.85	Peru, Ill.	800	2.25
Rome	850		12		= 4.20	Madison, Wis.	850	2.40
Stockholm	860		16	3	= 5.69	Montgomery, Ala.	860	3.05
Warsaw	875		13	3	= 4.64	St. Louis, Mo.	880	2.00
Pesth	880		12	3	= 4.29	Galena, Ill.	880	2.35
Cagliari	925		14		= 4.90	Rock Island, Ill.	900	2.35
Naples	950		11		= 3.85	Prairie du Chien, Wis.	950	2.65
Lisbon	955		14		= 4.90	Quincy, Ill.	950	2.60
Seville	980		13		= 4.55	Jefferson City, Mo.	975	2.70
Cadiz	1,000		13		= 4.55	Mobile, Ala.	1,000	3.00
Belgrade	1,005		13	6	= 4.72	Little Rock, Ark.	1,050	4.00
Palermo	1,080		12		= 4.20	Des Moines, Iowa.	1,080	2.70
St. Petersburg	1,160		18	6	= 6.47	New Orleans, La.	1,100	3.25
Novgorod	1,275		18	6	= 6.47	Houston, "	1,330	5.00
Smolensk	1,280		18	6	= 6.47	Galveston, Texas	1,340	3.95
Malta	1,250		16	9	= 5.87	Grand Island, Nebraska	1,350	4.60
Odessa	1,360		18	6	= 6.47	Fort Kearney, "	1,380	5.25
Athens	1,450	1	12		= 11.36	Austin, Texas	1,460	5.50
Constantinople	1,480		19	6	= 7.00	San Antonio, Texas	1,550	5.50
Smyrna	1,540	1	6	6	= 9.43	Fort Laramie, Nebraska	1,600	6.40
Nishni Novgorod	1,700	1	2		= 7.86	Denver, Colorado	1,700	7.60
Moscow	1,485		19		= 6.65	Salt Lake City, Utah	2,100	5.95
Taganrog	1,490	1	6		= 9.26	Sacramento, California	2,500	6.75
Sjumen	1,500	1	8		= 9.96	Stockton, "	2,500	6.75
Alexandria *	1,867	2	6	9	= 16.69	San Francisco, "	2,600	6.75

MORE ERRONEOUS STATEMENTS.

Mr. Hubbard's assertion that, " where a message is repeated, the expense is increased about seventy-five per cent, but on well-constructed lines, in ordinary weather, messages between any two stations east of a line from St. Paul to New Orleans require but one repetition," hardly needs refutation. East of the line named there are more than four thousand telegraph offices, and at least 1,300 separate and distinct circuits. How, then, can separate wires be maintained between every two stations over this vast territory? Even confining the statement to one office at the East, — say Boston, for example, — how is it possible to maintain separate circuits that will enable that office to work direct with each one of four thousand offices? It would be more practicable to travel from every town in the United States to every other town, without change of cars, than it would to establish *direct* telegraphic connection between each.

The Western Union Telegraph Company maintains independent circuits, and works direct between New York and Philadelphia, Washington, Boston, Buffalo, Montreal, Chicago, Cincinnati, New Orleans, Portland, Plaister Cove, and many other points; but to work with every office in the United States without repetition would require more wires upon each pole than the mythical Briareus had hands.

SINGULAR NOTIONS OF PRACTICAL TELEGRAPHY.

It seems scarcely worth while to follow Mr. Hubbard in his statements regarding the capital of the Western Union Telegraph Company, and the cost of its lines. We have given a statement on pages 37 to 40 of the organization of this company, the amount of its capital, length of lines, and other matters of interest.

Mr. Hubbard's statement that the directors of the Western Union Telegraph Company have steadfastly refused to reduce rates until forced by competition, and then consolidated with the competing company, and again raised the rates, is without the slightest foundation in fact. We have previously stated that no increase in the rates has been made since the consolidation with the United States and American companies, but, on the contrary, they have been reduced to more than one thousand stations, while the opposition have less than three hundred offices all told.

ABSURD THEORIES REGARDING THE WORKING CAPACITY OF TELEGRAPH LINES.

Mr. Hubbard says : —

"The capacities of the line of telegraph are very great. 2,000 words an hour are easily transmitted by a good operator over a single wire. At this rate there could be sent over fifty-one of the eighty or ninety wires leading from the New York office of the Western Union Telegraph Company 2,448,000 words, or 97,920 messages of twenty-five words each, a day. This amount cannot be obtained. Forty messages an hour are easily transmitted by a good operator over a through line, and this number could be sent every hour by relays of operators. This estimate gives 1,224,000 words, or 48,960 messages. On through and local lines a deduction of one half for twelve hours of the day, during which the local lines are open, must be made, — 918,000 words, or 36,720 messages, on through and local lines. The average number actually transmitted on these fifty-one wires is 184,378 words, or 7,375 messages. 733,622 more words, or 29,340 more messages might daily be transmitted over these lines. If the present business could be distributed over all the hours of the day, or if there were sufficient business for all the wires the whole day, the rates could be largely reduced.

"Nearly eighteen hours of each day the wires are idle, yet a considerable portion of the expenses of the line are no greater than they would be if messages were transmitted the whole time. Interest, depreciation, and repairs, office rent, salaries, and general management are the same, whether much or little business is transacted. These items constitute about one third of all the expenses on the Western Union line. The other expenses will not be increased in proportion to the increase of the time."

In reply to the above, we assert that 2,000 words an hour are not easily transmitted by a good operator over a single wire. There are operators who can send at this rate for a short time, but they are very few in number, and none of them could maintain this rate of speed for any length of time. It must be recollected that a message must be copied with a pen as rapidly as it is sent. Now, we doubt if Mr. Hubbard even can write 2,000 words legibly within an hour, with pen and ink. It is well known that the celebrated horse Dexter has trotted a mile in the unpre-

cedented time of 2.17, but would it not be absurd to state, on
that account, that every good horse can easily trot twenty-six miles
an hour? Why, Dexter himself cannot keep up this rate of speed
for even a quarter of an hour. Because a celebrated pedestrian
walked a hundred miles in twenty-four hours, would it be just to
say that every good walker can easily walk 36,500 miles per
annum? A man in California rode three hundred miles in
twenty-four hours; would it be honest, therefore, to say that every
good horseman can easily ride 9,000 miles a month? The
maximum speed of the best operators is 1,500 words per hour, but
the average speed of the best is very much below this.

The amount of business done upon a wire in a given time is
vastly greater in this country than in any other. In Europe there
are 355,218 miles of wire, while in the United States there are
less than one third as many, and yet the wires in this country
transmit more telegraphic matter per annum than all the lines in
Europe. This almost incredible fact is explained by the superior
character and ability of our operating staff. In Europe they still
use recording instruments, and slowly and laboriously pick out
their messages upon strips of paper. Here, on the contrary, every
operator — except in the small villages — reads by sound, and
does three times as much work upon a wire as the poorly paid and
inefficient European operator. Now, this being the case, — and the
statistics prove it, — it can hardly be pretended that our company
gets much less out of its wires than they can reasonably perform,
and yet Mr. Hubbard says we " could easily send on fifty-one
wires 97,920 messages per day, while in reality we only send
7,375." Here is a difference between theory and practice that
beats even Dexter's 2.17 as the rate of speed which every
horse in America can average.

IMPOSSIBILITY OF UTILIZING THE TELEGRAPH LINES BY NIGHT AS WELL AS DAY.

Mr. Hubbard says, " If the present business could be distributed over all the hours of the day, or if there were sufficient
business for all the wires the whole day, the rates could be largely
reduced "; but neither of these propositions can be realized. The
telegraph is an errand-boy which every one uses when the exi-

gency requires it, and which no one will use unnecessarily, even though it **work** for nothing. **In order to** utilize the wires during those portions **of the** day and night when they are comparatively idle, the Western **Union** Telegraph Company adopted the following rates for night messages : —

" This company will transmit messages between **the** principal cities on its lines east of St. Louis and New Orleans, both **in-**clusive, during the night, and deliver the same **the** succeeding morning, on the following terms : **For** a message of 20 words or less, the usual tolls on a ten-word **message** will be **charged.** For a message of more than 20 words, and not exceeding 60 words, twice the usual tolls **on a ten-word message** will be charged. For **a** message of **more than 60 words, and not** exceeding 120 words, three times **the usual tolls on a** ten-word message will **be** charged. For **each additional** 100 words, **or** part thereof, in excess of 120 **words, the usual** tolls on a ten-word message will be charged in **addition.** Such messages will be known as NIGHT MESSAGES. They will be received for transmission at any time during the day **or** evening, **and** will **be sent during the** succeeding night. *No additional charge will be made for cipher messages.*"

The very moderate success **of our** night-message **experiment,** notwithstanding the large inducements **offered,** proves **that the use of the** telegraph is required **not merely** for communication, but for emergency and despatch. It is also a fact worthy of notice, that very little of **this** business **is** done between Boston, New York, Philadelphia, Baltimore, and Washington, notwithstanding **the** low rates, whereby over a hundred words can be transmitted for a dollar. **It is done mainly between remote** places like Chicago, Milwaukee, **St. Louis, Cincinnati, Memphis, and New** Orleans, communication **between which by mail requires from two** to four days.

In support **of** this theory we submit a statement of the night-message business between New York City and all points on our **lines for** the months of March, July, and October. These months **represent fairly** the varying phases of our business in respect to **trade** in different sections of the country at different seasons of the **year.**

The total number of night **messages** sent and received between

New York City and all places on our lines for the three months named was 6,273, divided as follows : —

Between New York and	Charleston, S. C.	.	.	. 276
" " "	Chicago, Ill.	.	.	. 904
" " "	Cincinnati, O.	.	.	. 326
" " "	St. Louis, Mo.	.	.	433
" " "	Milwaukee, Wis.	.	.	. 176
" " "	Memphis, Tenn. .	.	.	316
" " "	Montgomery, Ala. .	.	.	. 176
" " "	Mobile, Ala.	.	.	. 402
" " "	New Orleans, La. .	.	.	. 1,195
" " "	All other places .	.	.	. 2,069
Total,	. .	. .	. .	. 6,273

Our night-message experiment has proved that the telegraph will not be used at night, at any tariff, except to a moderate extent and between distant points.

The absurdity of placing the telegraph and postal systems in the same category has been fully shown on pages 43 and 44. Mr. Hubbard appears to have read Mr. Scudamore's charges against the English system, and applied them literally to the telegraphs of this country. Unfortunately, however, charges which may be true as applied to the companies operating the telegraphs in the United Kingdom have no pertinency when reproduced as the shortcomings of the American system.

PROPOSED INCORPORATION OF THE UNITED STATES POSTAL TELEGRAPH COMPANY.

Mr. Hubbard says : —

"It is not considered expedient either for the government to purchase the existing lines, or to construct and operate lines. How, then, can the desired results be best attained? The Post-Office Department has no facilities of its own for the transmission of correspondence either by rail or telegraph. It contracts with the railroad companies for carrying the mail, and it is proposed that it shall contract with a telegraph company for transmitting messages.

"A bill was introduced at the last session of Congress, and referred to the committee on Post Roads and Routes, to incorporate the 'United States Postal Telegraph Company, and to establish a postal system.'

" **The first,** second, third, fourth, **and fifth** sections of the bill in-**corporate the** company, with **power to construct** lines on all the post roads and routes of the country.

" The sixth section authorizes the Postmaster-General to receive **bids** from any telegraph company for the transmission by telegraph **of** messages received and delivered through the post-office, to all cities and villages of 5,000 inhabitants and over, and to towns on **the** line of the telegraph, where stations may be established by order of the Postmaster-General.

" The seventh section authorizes the Postmaster-General to con-tract for the transmission by telegraph **of** messages **with** the company that will engage to transmit **them for** the least sum, provided such sum does not exceed **twenty-five** cents, including five **cents** postage for each message **of twenty words,** including **date,** address, and signature, **for each and every 500** miles or fractional part thereof the message **may be transmitted, with** five cents for each added five words. **All messages to be** prepaid by stamps, or written on **stamped paper.**

" **Messages to** be received at any and all post-offices, street-boxes, **or** other **receptacles for** letters, and to be delivered by special car-**rier** without extra expense.

" Messages requiring immediate **despatch to have priority of** transmission on payment of extra rates.

" The effect of the proposed reduction **will be** better appreciated by comparing the present and proposed rates.

DISTANCES.	Present Rates.	Proposed Rates.	Reduction.	Pro Rata Reduction.
To stations within 500 miles	$0.41	$0.30	$0.11	26 per ct.
" " between 500 and 1,000 miles .	1.43	0.55	0.88	62 "
" " between 1,000 and 1,500 miles .	2.41	0.81	1.60	67 "
" " between 1,500 and 2,000 miles .	3.41	1.47	1.94	56 "
Averages	$1.00;	$0.47;	$0.53;	53 "

MESSAGES DELIVERED WITHIN A MILE OF THE OFFICE FREE.

The rule was established coincident with **the** introduction of **the telegraph in** the United **States** to deliver **all** messages in the **town within a mile** of the receiving office free. Special and free **delivery should be** the rule **as far** as practicable. And yet it is impossible, **without** rendering **the** telegraph of no avail in im-**portant** emergencies, to establish **free** delivery everywhere. A **message from an** Eastern city to **a Western village** announcing peril, disaster, or death is addressed to a person two or three miles from the telegraph station. The charge for transmitting this message is, say, fifty cents. Two modes of delivery are presented, — one to drop it in the post-office, where it may lie until the next day ; the other, to hire a conveyance, and send a special messenger with it to the person addressed. The cost of this special service will vary from one dollar to two dollars. Our practice is to deliver by special messenger, and charge therefor the actual cost of the service.

EUROPEAN CHARGES FOR DELIVERING TELEGRAMS.

A similar custom prevails in Europe, as will appear from the following extracts from the rules and regulations applicable to stations in the Austro-Germanic Telegraph Union, which comprises Austria, Prussia, Hanover, Holland, Saxony, Wurtemburg, the German Duchies, also France and the whole South of Europe :

CHARGES FOR POSTAGE, FOOT MESSENGER, AND ESTAFETTE.

The instruction for forwarding despatches beyond Telegraph lines must be inserted in messages immediately after receiver's address and charged for ; messages with no instructions will be sent on from Terminal Telegraph Station by post.

The sender is responsible for an insufficient address, and can only rectify the same by sending and paying for a new despatch.

By Post (as Registered Letter) to all places in Europe, . . 0s. 10d.
"   "   to all other places, ... 2s. 0d.

Messages addressed to " Poste Restante " are subjected to the above charges for postage.

By Express (Foot Messenger) within seven English miles, 2s. 6d.

By Estafette (Mounted Messenger) a charge must be made at the rate of 2s. 6d. per three English miles for countries comprised in the Austro-Germanic Union, but for other towns the charge is 1s. 6d. per English mile. If, however, the distance is unknown, a sufficient deposit must be taken.

All charges to be prepaid by sender.

TELEGRAMS TO BE PLACED IN THE STREET BOXES.

Mr. Hubbard's proposition to put telegrams into street-boxes is simply absurd. Telegrams are always of an important nature, and need despatch. Imagine a message announcing sickness, death, or any other circumstance, being dropped in the street-box, to be taken out when the carrier happens round! As for post-offices, how many are there in any of the large cities even? Few have more than one, and this is closed when a mail arrives, — a circumstance that seems to have rendered the closed condition the normal one with many post-offices.

To give an idea of the extent of present facilities in the principal cities, the following statement, showing the number of telegraph offices now open, is submitted : —

New York, ...	100 offices.
Philadelphia, ...	35 "
Baltimore, ...	19 "
Washington, ...	16 "
Boston, ...	24 "
Chicago, ...	22 "
Cincinnati, ...	21 "

PRIVILEGED PERSONS TO HAVE PRIORITY IN THE USE OF THE WIRES.

Mr. Hubbard's plan of allowing " messages requiring immediate despatch to have priority of transmission on payment of extra rates," would abolish the rule which has always been observed since the establishment of the telegraph in this country, " first come first served," and give privileged persons the priority in the use of the wires. What an excellent opportunity this would afford speculative combinations (like that which locked up twenty millions of currency in Wall Street a short time ago) to extend their operations all over the country, by practically controlling the telegraph?

This plan would not answer at all. No system of variation of rate is feasible, consistently with public policy, but that which offers a lower rate for business which will consent to be delayed until another day.

In regard to the establishment of a money-order system by telegraph, we would say that we have long done something in the way of transmitting deposits and money orders by telegraph. We have made no effort to bring it prominently before the public, with a view to extending this department of our business, for the reason that as an established system it would be comparatively easy for rogues to abuse it. It is only resorted to in cases of great emergency, where money orders by post cannot be delivered in time to meet the necessities of the case. It is also confined mainly to the transmission of small sums. It involves necessarily the sending of two messages. Large amounts required in commercial transactions are daily transmitted or exchanged in this manner by the regular banking houses in all the principal cities.

PROPOSITION TO OPERATE TELEGRAPHS AT A LOSS, AND MAKE MONEY BY IT.

Mr. Hubbard proposes, by his new plan, to send telegrams at an average reduction of 53 per cent from the present charges, which we have shown to be 25 per cent less than the European rates. Now, the total receipts of the Western Union Telegraph Company for the year ending June 30, 1867, were $6,568,925, and a reduction of 53 per cent would leave $3,087,405.

The working expenses for the year were	$3,944,005
Receipts with Mr. Hubbard's proposed tariff,	3,087,405
Loss for the year	$856,600

Mr. Hubbard acknowledges that neither the government nor any company can transmit messages at the above rates without loss, but claims that "a company with well-constructed lines, *built for cash,* can transmit messages at these rates, in connection with the post-office, and realize a large profit." Precisely how this is to be done, or what the lines "built for cash" have got to do about it, does not appear. Mr. Hubbard says in his pamphlet that "the largest part of the lines of the Western Union Company were constructed before the rise in prices, and on a gold basis." Now, if he means that lines built on a paper basis can be worked cheaper than those constructed on a gold one, we would be glad to hear his reasons for so singular a notion.

SPECULATIVE TELEGRAPH SCHEMES.

We consider it our duty to say a word concerning the swarm of adventurers who are canvassing the country for subscriptions to utterly worthless telegraph stock, and who are besieging the halls of Congress every year for some recognition or advantage which shall enable them the more readily to impose upon the public.

The National Telegraph Company is an example in point. This concern, which claims to have organized two years ago under an act of Congress, and which has filled the country with runners begging for subscriptions to its stock, has never set a pole.

The losses which have occurred in the operation of competing lines are enormous. The country is full of people who have lost money in these schemes, which, after a brief existence, are wound up and their effects disposed of by the sheriff.

The present condition of all the opposition lines is very precarious. The Franklin Company was made by a consolidation of the Insulated Company, having four wires between Boston and Washington, and the old Franklin Company, having two wires between Boston and New York. The capital of the former was $1,250,000, and of the latter $500,000. The new organization has been in operation about two years, during which time its receipts have fallen so far below its expenses that it has contracted a debt of $125,000; and its lines have deteriorated to such an extent that a large sum would have to be expended to put them in proper condition for business. The stock of such companies is valueless as an investment, and, in respect to some of them, it is doubtful if their property could be sold for a sum sufficient to pay their indebtedness.

The Atlantic and Pacific Company has a line from New York to Chicago, via Albany, Buffalo, Cleveland, and Sandusky, averaging about two wires for each line. Its lines are built under a contract to take stock in payment, at the rate of $1,666.66 per mile for a line of two wires.

The operation of these separate and irresponsible lines, during the brief period of their existence, retards the progress of legitimate telegraphy, and impairs the general unity of the system. Any legislation of Congress which is made to further such schemes has the direct effect of aiding a class of speculators to fleece a credulous public, by inducing them to invest their money in the construction of lines which never have paid, and never can pay, the expenses of operating them, and which are of no benefit to any persons but those who originate them, and profit by their construction.

MORE STARTLING INVENTIONS FOR RAPID TELEGRAPHING.

We quote from Mr. Hubbard: —

"Instruments have been recently invented, and are in operation, either in England or in this country, by which two great hindrances to the efficiency of the telegraph are remedied. Mr. Stearns, president of the Franklin Telegraph Company, has invented an instrument by which messages are transmitted both ways at the same time, on the same wire, thus doubling its capacity without any increase of expense. Sir Charles Wheatstone, in England, has invented an instrument by which double the number of words can be transmitted and received on the same wire, at an increased expense in the preparation of the message for transmission. Instruments are also in operation in Great Britain, worked by boys, after instruction of one or two days."

In regard to Mr. Stearns's apparatus for working both ways over one wire at the same time, we are compelled to say there is nothing new in the idea. Doctor Gintl, of Germany, invented it many years ago, and it was published in an Italian work,* with steel-plate illustration, issued in 1861, translated into English by George B. Prescott, of Albany, and published in the Telegraphic Journal, London, May, 1864. Moses G. Farmer, Esq., of Boston, invented another apparatus for doing the same thing, and worked it between Boston and Portland, in 1849. If there is any practical value in this apparatus it is open — like the Morse Telegraph — to the use of all. Sir Charles Wheatstone's apparatus, by which double the number of words can be received on the same wire, will probably prove of the same practical value as

* Manuale di Telegrafia Elettrica, di Carlo Matteucci, Torino, 1861.

many similar inventions, which in theory can transmit intelligence with the greatest accuracy at the astonishing rate of five or ten thousand words an hour, but in practice have never proved of the slightest value.

It is suggestive, that, of more than a hundred inventions designed to supersede the Morse telegraph, the latter instrument is used to-day on more than 490,000 miles of wire out of the total of 500,000 in operation in all parts of the world. Mr. Hubbard's assertion, " that instruments are in operation in Great Britain, worked by boys, after instruction of one or two days," may be true. From all accounts, the use of boys — and charity boys at that — has been the great curse of telegraphy in England, until the saying has become common there, when describing a remarkably poor specimen of chirography, that "it is written as badly as a telegraph despatch." We hope the day is far distant when our messages shall be transmitted by boys with one or two days' instruction.

We hardly need say that it is for our interest to adopt every improvement whereby the despatch of business within a given time can be materially increased. It is certainly cheaper for us to provide new instruments, at almost any cost which will ever be charged therefor, than to put up, keep in repair, and operate additional wires to produce the same results.

ERRONEOUS TABLE OF EUROPEAN STATISTICS.

We reproduce Mr. Hubbard's statistical table for the purpose of pointing out some very serious errors contained in it.

				In U. S. Gold.			In U. S. Gold.*
The Austrian florin is rated by Mr. Hubbard at			$ 0.41		True value		$0.48
Franc	"	"	"	.20	"	"	.19
£ Sterling	"	"	"	4.84	"	"	4.86
Lira	"	"	"	$.18\frac{6}{10}$	"	"	.19
Dollar of Norway	"	"	"	.53	"	"	1.09
Rouble	"	"	"	$.21\frac{3}{7}$	"	"	$.77\frac{1}{2}$
Dollar of Spain	"	"	"	1.00	"	"	$1.04\frac{1}{2}$

* We are indebted for the estimation of the value of these foreign coins in United States gold to E. B. Elliott, Esq., of Washington, D. C., who has recently prepared a valuable work on the subject.

These errors, in reducing foreign money into United States gold currency caused the following discrepancies in gross receipts for the year : —

	Value in United States Gold, according to Table.	True Value in United States Gold.	Difference.
Austria,	$ 674,344	$ 789,476.16	$ 115,132.16
England,	2,481,500	2,491,756.02	10,256.02
Italy,	766,750	' 782,859.09	16.109.09
Norway,	182,131	374,573.15	192,442.15
Russia,	372,309	1,451,310.72	1,079,001.72
Spain,	554,475	576,654.00	22,179.00
	Discrepancy,		$ 1,435,120.14
France,	1,541,518	1,464,442.10	77,075.90
Belgium,	194,442	182,611.28	11,830.72
Bavaria,	136,894	132,383.26	4.510.74
	Discrepancy,		$ 93,417.36

Thus we find that in reproducing from their various currencies the gross telegraphic receipts of six nations into United States gold, Mr. Hubbard makes the amount $ 1,435,120.14 less than it should be, and in reducing those of three other countries into our coin he makes the amount $ 93,417.36 more than it should be.

He has also failed to give the receipts of the three great Submarine Telegraph Companies, which transact so important an amount of continental telegraph business.

Mr. Hubbard gives the number of stations in Switzerland at 333, while the best English authority * gives it at 252. He also gives the number of messages transmitted in England, in 1866, as 6,127,000, while Mr. Scudamore, in his reply to the statement of the Electric and International Telegraph Company, published in May, 1868,† points out the fact that only 5,781,189 messages were transmitted throughout Great Britain and Ireland during that year.

It will be observed that Mr. Hubbard has " estimated " — that is, guessed at — the number of and receipts for telegrams in the Netherlands, Denmark, Sweden, Turkey, and Greece. He estimates the average cost per message to be 42 cents; but as we happen to know that the average cost in Denmark was more than twice this amount, we are not willing to accept any of his estimates.

* Government and the Telegraphs. London, 1868.

† Return to an order of the Honorable the House of Commons for copy of further correspondence between the Treasury and the Postmaster-General relating to the Electric Telegraphs Bill.

ERRONEOUS TABLE OF EUROPEAN STATISTICS.

From Mr. Hubbard's pamphlet:—

Statistics of the Telegraph in Europe for the Year 1866.

NAME OF COUNTRY.	Number of Stations.	Miles of Wire.	Rates in 1866.	Number of Messages.	Receipts.			
England	2,151	80,466	1 shilling.	6,127,000	£ sterling	512,707 ×	$4.84 =	$2,481,500.00
France	1,209	68,687	½ and 1 franc.	2,842,554	Francs	7,707,590 ×	0.20 =	1,541,518.00
Austria	851	73,854	. . .	2,507,472	Florins	1,644,742 ×	0.41 =	674,344.00
Prussia	538	55,149	. . .	1,964,003	Thalers	1,275,785 ×	0.72 =	918,565.00
Belgium	356	6,146	¼ franc.	1,128,005	Francs	961,112 ×	0.20 =	194,442.00
Switzerland	333	3,717	½ franc.	668,916	"	684,471 ×	0.20 =	136,894.00
Bavaria	. . .	4,945	. . .	. . .	Florins	322,876 ×	0.41 =	132,383.00
Norway	73	2,710	. . .	269,375	Rix Dolls.	343,645 ×	0.53 =	182,131.00
Russia	368	37,330	. . .	838,653	Roubles	1,872,659 ×	0.21¼ =	372,309.00
Italy	529	22,214	. . .	1,760,889	Lira	4,120,311 ×	0.18 6/16 =	766,750.00
Spain	. . .	. . .	. . .	633,376	Dollars	554,475 ×	1.00 =	554,475.00
Netherlands	. . .	. . .	. . .	. . .	. . .			
Denmark	. . .	. . .	. . .	1,500,000	. . .	×	0.42 =	630,000.00
Sweden	. . .	. . .	. . .					
Turkey	. . .	. . .	. . .					
Greece	. . .	. . .	. . .					
Total messages				18,640,243	Total receipts			$8,585,311.00
Average rate per message in Europe								$0.42

EUROPEAN TELEGRAMS COUNTED SEVERAL TIMES.

An examination of Mr. Hubbard's statement of the number of messages sent in Europe, in 1866, will reveal the fact that he has included inland, international, and transit messages to make up the grand total. In this way he has counted the same message several times. For instance, messages sent from England to France, or any two contiguous countries, would be counted in each. Messages between France and Germany would be counted in France and Germany as international messages, and in Belgium and perhaps some other country as transit. The same would be the case between all European countries whose territories do not border on each other. A message going from France to Russia, or from England to Turkey, might be counted a dozen times.

In the United States each message is counted but once, although it may traverse thousands of miles in reaching its place of destination.

We have not the statistics to show what proportion the legitimate number of messages sent bears to this fictitious number; but by referring to the Belgian table it will be seen that 692,536 inland and 306,596 international messages were sent in 1866, in a total of 1,128,005. Taking this as a fair average for the whole of Europe, we shall find that only 14,012,795 messages were sent in 1866, at an expense, in United States currency, of $15,286,911.61, or about $1.09 each.

LABOR THE PRINCIPAL ELEMENT OF EXPENSE IN OPERATING TELEGRAPHS.

The principal element of expense in our business is the cost of labor.* If we can do our work as cheaply as another party, it is clear that rates can never be reduced below the point at which receipts and expenses are equal. Any material increase of business, no matter what the rates may be, must be attended with increased expense. And when the capacity of the wires provided for a par-

* The Western Union Telegraph Company expended $2,573,434.80 for labor for the year ending June 30, 1867. See comparison of cost of labor in Europe and the United States on page 26.

ticular service is exhausted, a new question is presented by the necessity for providing additional facilities. By the extension of our lines this year west of Chicago, and by the moderate increase in the volume of our business in that section of the country, it will probably become necessary during next year to provide two additional wires between Chicago and the Atlantic coast. The cost of these wires, if erected on poles now standing, will be about $120,000. We shall also be obliged to put up an additional wire between Washington and New Orleans, and between the latter place and Louisville. The cost of maintaining the lines will be somewhat increased by the addition of these wires, and the cost of operating at each end, and looking after them at intermediate points, must also be included. How is the additional capital necessary to provide such increased facilities to be raised? By reducing rates, the result of which is, that, even if gross receipts are not diminished, the expenses are increased? Is it not by gradually increasing lines out of current profits, and as gradually reducing rates after facilities for an enlarged business have been provided?

PREVAILING ERROR OF ALL THEORIZERS ON THE BUSINESS OF TELEGRAPHING.

All theorizers upon the subject of the telegraph fall into the error that the amount of business which may be done at any point (the rates being low enough) is in the ratio of population. An investigation of the subject will show this to be entirely erroneous. Three years ago, when the subject of telegraphic communication between the Eastern and Western continents was discussed by those most intimately connected with the enterprise, no one estimated the number of messages which would pass between the two continents, daily, at a rate of $50 gold for ten words, below 500. But few placed the figures so low. Most of them estimated the number at two or three times this minimum.

In 1863 Mr. Cyrus W. Field made the following remarks before the Chamber of Commerce of New York, in relation to the probable amount of business that would be done between Europe and America when communication by telegraph should be established : " To express my own opinion, from pretty large experience on the subject, I do not believe that *ten* cables would begin to do the work which would, in a short time, be given to it."

At the banquet given in London, in 1864, to inaugurate the renewed attempt by the Atlantic Telegraph Company to unite Europe and America by means of the Atlantic cable, Mr. Cromwell F. Varley made the following remarks touching the amount of business that would be offered for transmission over the cable: "I feel great confidence that, when once a cable is successfully laid across the Atlantic, the demands upon it will be so great that you will have to lay one or two per annum for the next twenty years, or even more."

Their disappointment was, therefore, very great when, after the Atlantic Cable was in operation, it was found that the daily average at the $100 tariff was but 29 messages, and at the $50 tariff, which was in operation thirteen months, it was but 64. At the $25 rate the average advanced to 131; and although the rate has been still further reduced to $16.85, the average is but 201. This illustration is sufficient to prove the fallacy of all reasoning concerning telegraph business based merely upon population. We venture the prediction that, at the rate of $5 between Europe and America, the number of messages which would pass per day would never equal the number exchanged daily between New York on one hand, and Philadelphia and Boston on the other. The reason is simply this: The number of messages which will pass within a given time between two points depends, first, upon a reasonable charge for transmission,—a charge conveniently within the means of those having occasion to communicate; and secondly and mainly, upon the number of people at either extreme having intimate business relations with those at the other. The vast commerce of the Old World and the New is not exchanged in detail, but in bulk. A few banking-houses on each side make all the exchanges for both continents, and the agricultural products and the manufactures of both are also exchanged in substantially the same manner.

We have shown how fallacious is the claim that the increase of business is dependent upon the tariff, by the statistics of our own and foreign countries, by which it appears that business has sometimes largely increased at an advanced rate. We do not desire to be understood, however, as saying that low tariffs, under similar circumstances, will not bring more business than high ones. But we do say that it is susceptible of proof, that the minimum rate is undoubtedly much higher than most of those who theorize upon this subject are willing to believe. Take the case of the Atlantic Cable as an illustration. During the three months at which the tariff was $100, and the daily average of messages 29, the receipts per day were £505. During the thirteen months, at the average of 64 messages daily, the receipts were £579. During the nine months, at the average of 131 messages per day, the receipts were £635. And for the two months since the rates were reduced to $16, the daily average has been 201 messages, and the average receipts £596.

Now it happens, fortunately for the Cable Company, that the present volume of business is considerably less than the capacity of their cables; so that the increase of that business has been attended with but a very slight additional expense, the cost to operate being the same at offices open day and night, whether operators are occupied all or only a part of the time. But suppose, for illustration, that the limit of the capacities of the cables will be reached when the average number of messages per day is 250. To undertake to transmit any number beyond this without further facilities would result in crowding and confusing the business to an extent which would inevitably produce dissatisfaction. On the other hand, to provide an additional cable would cost a sum of money which it might be exceedingly difficult to raise. It seems proper, therefore, that the profits from this business should always be considerably more than enough to yield a proper return for the capital invested, so that greater facilities may be provided out of surplus profits; and, as facilities are increased, rates may be gradually reduced, until, by judiciously pursuing this course, the charges for telegraphing may be materially diminished, without endangering the revenues to which owners of telegraph property are justly entitled.

Statistics of Traffic through the Atlantic Cables from July 28, 1866, *to November* 1, 1868.

Number of Messages per Month.	Daily Average No. of Messages.	Gross Amount of Receipts accruing to the Two Atlantic Cables, between Valentia and Heart's Content.							Average Amount per Day.
1,104 837 831	29	From July 28th to 31st Aug., 1866, under £20 Tariff " Sept. 1st " 30th " Oct. 1st " 31st			" "	" "	*£500 456 491		£505
1,530 1,582 1,686 1,764 2,147 2,624 2,262 1,843 1,432 1,693 1,800 2,506 2,292	64	" Nov. 1st " 30th " Dec. 1st " 31st " Jan. 1st " 31st " Feb. 1st " 28th " March 1st " 31st " April 1st " 30th " May 1st " 31st " June 1st " 30th " July 1st " 27th " July 18th " 31st Aug. " Sept. 1st " 30th " Oct. 1st " 31st " Nov. 1st " 30th	1867	£10	" " " " " " " " " " " " "	† 502 498 466 549 666 722 705 597 542 401 515 715 661		£579
3,901 4,739 5,128 4,507 4,320 3,538 2,884 3,217 3,740	131	" Dec. 1st " 31st " Jan. 1st " 31st " Feb. 1st " 29th " March 1st " 31st " April 1st " 30th " May 1st " 31st " June 1st " 30th " July 1st " 31st " Aug. 1st " 31st	1868	£5.5	" " " " " " " " "	‡ 732 756 860 707 718 550 447 490 553		£635
5,053 6,341 6,877	201	" Sept. 1st " 30th " Oct. 1st " 31st " Nov. 1st " 30th		£3.7.6.	" " "	591 615 670		£596

A single wire between New York and Plaister Cove, Cape Breton, the eastern terminus of the Western Union Telegraph Company's lines, not only promptly transmits all the telegraphic business that is done between Europe and America, but every message is telegraphed back for comparison with the original, to insure correctness.

* During this month over £100 per day were paid by the New York Herald for news reports, and many persons sent messages as a novelty.

† During this month the despatches sent by the United States government averaged over £100 per day.

‡ During these months there was extraordinary excitement in cotton.

PROGRESS

ELECTRIC TELEGRAPH IN AMERICA AND EUROPE.

THE UNITED STATES.

THE United States not only has the distinguished honor of being the birthplace of the inventor of the universally-used electric telegraph, but of having constructed the first line of practical telegraph, and of being the foremost nation in the world, at the present time, in the number of her telegraph stations, extent of her lines and wires, cheapness of her rates, and amount of business done.

The United States contains 4,126 telegraph offices; 62,782 miles of line; 125,564 miles of wire; and transmits annually 12,904,777 telegrams.

She has nearly as many telegraph stations as, and sends a greater number of telegrams annually than, all Continental Europe, and contains as many miles of line as Belgium, Bavaria, France, Great Britain and Ireland, Italy, Russia, Switzerland, and Spain combined.

PROPORTION OF TELEGRAMS TO LETTERS.

The proportion of telegrams to letters in the United States is difficult of determination, from the fact that our Post-Office Department furnishes no statistics of the number of letters sent through the mails, and has no means of ascertaining the number approximately, except by the number of stamps sold annually. This mode of estimation is very defective, because the stamps sold may not have been used, or if used, may have covered the postage on books, parcels, and other matter. The Postmaster-General states, in his report for 1867, that there were 283,762,300 three-cent stamps sold during the preceding year. Supposing each of these stamps to represent a letter, we have the following comparative result of the number of telegrams to letters in the various countries where the telegraph is most extensively used : —

					Proportion of telegrams to letters in the United Kingdom,	.	1 to 121
"	"	"	"	"	" Switzerland,	. . .	1 to 69
"	"	"	"	"	" Belgium,	. . . .	1 to 37
"	"	"	"	"	" United States,	. . .	1 to 22

EARLY HISTORY OF THE TELEGRAPH IN AMERICA.

During the first few years after the introduction of the electric telegraph its progress was very slow. Capitalists were afraid to invest in an undertaking so novel and precarious, and as a natural consequence there was great difficulty in raising funds for properly building the lines, and they were constructed in a very unreliable manner, breaks and interruptions being rather the normal condition of the wires than the exception.

At a very early period in the history of the electric telegraph in the United States, a misunderstanding occurred between the Morse patentees and a contractor under them, the result of which was that rival lines were constructed throughout the country before the system had been sufficiently developed to be remunerative, even without such competition.

The invention of the letter-printing telegraph by Mr. House, in 1846, and the introduction of the electro-chemical telegraph of Mr. Bain into this country, in 1849, greatly facilitated the construction of competing lines.

The first line operating under the House patent was completed in March, 1849, from Philadelphia to New York City. The Boston and New York Telegraph Company, using the same patent, was completed in the autumn of the same year, and was followed by one from New York to Buffalo, and subsequently to St. Louis and Chicago.

During the year 1849, which was very prolific in the production of competing lines, the Bain patent was introduced upon lines extending between New York and Buffalo, and New York and Washington, **and, in the succeeding year, upon** lines extending between Boston and **Montreal, and Boston and** Portland.

In 1851 there were seven Bain lines in operation in the United States, having over 2,000 miles of wire ; eight House lines, having about 300 miles of wire ; and sixty-seven Morse lines, having 20,000 miles of wire. In the autumn of this year, the Morse and Bain lines between New York and Washington were consolidated ; and in the succeeding spring the Morse and Bain lines between New York and Boston were united under one company. The union of these lines was followed by that **of the** New York and Buffalo Morse and Bain **lines, and subsequently by** those of the House lines between **these points.**

EVILS ARISING FROM SEPARATE ORGANIZATIONS.

The consolidation of these lines was a step in the right direction, as it increased the receipts and lessened the expenses of the companies, while it enabled them to **do the** business better, by possessing greater facilities. **Still,** the great number of separate organizations remaining throughout **the country prevented that** unity and despatch in the conduct of the business **so essential to its** success. Under these circumstances, the public failed to realize the brilliant thought of instant communication between distant points.

A Boston house, doing business with Chicago, was obliged to be content with **responses** received on the second or third day. **On Boston despatches for** Chicago four tariffs were charged ; and a message had to be copied off and **handed over** to **other compa**nies for transmission at New York, Buffalo, and Detroit, before it reached its destination.

All this process required time, and yet the loss **of** time was the least of the evils connected with such a state of things. The message, **as** it left the writer's hands in Boston, was not unfrequently a very different document when it reached the Western parties, owing to errors caused by its numerous retransmissions, and thus the necessity became urgent to unite these separate companies into one living, vigorous organization, by which not only repetition and error might be avoided, but the messages followed to their destination under a single direction, and undivided responsibility.

THE UNIFICATION OF THE TELEGRAPH ACCOMPLISHED.

It was at this period, when segregated lines were feeling their weakness, and their revenues were unequal to even a current vigorous support, that a few clear-sighted men in the West conceived the project of buying up the groups of feeble organizations, and making them direct leaders between the large Western cities. The stock was comparatively valueless, and easily and cheaply bought. The needs of commercial intercourse were pressing. The project had in it the true elements of success, and it was accomplished.

For seven years thereafter the purchasers went on improving the lines thus acquired, and rendering their connections more certain. During all these years no dividends were paid. Time and money and all the earnings of the line were devoted to that series of combinations which, from a mass of weak and perishing organizations, culminated in the Western Union Telegraph Company.

This combination of lines saved the system from disgrace, and made it available to commerce and to public wants. No increase of rates followed any of these movements; and none would ever have been made, had not war come to change values, and rendered it necessary.

At the East, the American Telegraph Company, organized in 1855, followed a similar course, and ultimately controlled lines extending throughout the Atlantic seaboard and Mississippi Valley. These two companies, working in connection and harmony, covered the entire area of the United States, and performed the business of telegraphing better than it had ever been done before.

In 1863 the United States Telegraph Company was organized, and constructed lines in the territories occupied by both the Western Union and American companies; but in 1865, with 16,000 miles of wire, — all newly built, — worked to their full capacity during the year they were unable to meet their current expenses; but under the most vigorous administration, with its expenses reduced within the closest limits, found that it was conducting its business at an average net loss of nearly $10,000 per month.

In the spring of 1866 the Western Union, American, and United States Telegraph Companies were consolidated, thus producing a complete unification of the great telegraphic system of the United States, and rendering it the most complete and extensive in the world. This consolidation, however, gave the Western Union Telegraph Company no monopoly of the business. The Morse patent having expired, and no exclusive privileges being granted by either State or national governments, the construction and operation of telegraph lines within the jurisdiction of the United States remained freely open to all.

TELEGRAPH COMPANIES IN THE UNITED STATES.

The following list of some of the more important telegraph companies now doing business in the United States will convey an idea of the importance of this interest : Bankers and Brokers' Telegraph Company, capital $1,050,000, lines extending from New York to Washington ; Pacific and Atlantic Telegraph Company, capital $3,000,000, lines completed from Philadelphia to Pittsburg and Cincinnati, and extending ; Franklin Telegraph Company, capital $1,000,000, lines extending from Boston to Washington ; International Telegraph Company, capital $300,000, lines completed from Boston to Bangor, Me., and will be extended farther east ; Keystone Telegraph Company, lines extending from Philadelphia to Harrisburg and Pittsburg ; International Ocean Telegraph Company, lines extending from Lake City to Key West and Havana ; Northern Telegraph Company, capital $100,000, lines completed from Boston to Bristol, N. H., and extending ; Atlantic and Pacific Telegraph Company, capital $5,000,000, lines completed from New York to Chicago and extending ; Great Western Telegraph Company, line completed between Chicago and Milwaukee ; Northwestern Telegraph Company, capital $1,150,000, lines extending from Milwaukee through Wisconsin, Michigan, Iowa, and Minnesota ; Mississippi Valley Telegraph Company, lines extending between St. Paul, Minn., and St. Louis, and from Dubuque to Chicago ; Western Union Telegraph Company, capital $40,347,700, lines extending from the Gulf of Mexico to the Gulf of the St. Lawrence, and from the Atlantic to the Pacific ocean. There are in addition to this list quite a large number of companies, covering more or less territory, which, with all of the above mentioned, are independent organizations, and nearly all of them engaged in competition with each other.

Private enterprise has with us, so far, achieved much greater results than governmental management in Europe. As regards the tariff for messages, they are less than the rates established in Europe. Considerable reductions have been made within the past year, amounting, in some cases, to as much as 50 per cent. The reductions have taken place to the greatest extent in those sections of the country where there are opposition lines, the rates over some of these routes being less than the expense of doing the business, but the reductions are not confined to these sections.

The Western Union Telegraph Company has reduced its rates between upwards of one thousand offices where there is no opposition ; and it is now preparing a new tariff of rates, based upon airline distances, between all stations, irrespective of the circuitous routes that the lines take to reach them, which will still farther simplify and cheapen the system.

It is the purpose of this company to do the telegraphing of the United States as well, and at as low rates, as it can be done by any organization which can be formed, and thus maintain its possession of the first and most extensive system of telegraphy in the world.

DOMINION OF CANADA.

In the Dominion of Canada as in the United States, the telegraph is free and untrammelled by governmental interference, and, next to the United States, is the best in the world.

STATISTICS OF THE TELEGRAPH IN THE DOMINION OF CANADA.

Number of miles of pole line,	6,746 miles.
Number of miles of wire strung,	8,935 "
Number of offices,	382 "
Number of messages (in 1867),	573,219 "
Gross receipts from all sources,	$ 258,000
Gross expenses,	180,000
Of which, accruing for labor,	105,000

AUSTRIA.

The telegraph is under the control and management of the State.

At the end of 1866 the system comprised 851 stations, with an extent of 73,854 geographical miles of wire.

The total number of persons employed by the telegraphic department is 1,884.

TABLE C.

Statement showing the Progress of Telegraphy in Austria.

DATE.	Number of Messages.	Gross Receipts in Florins.	Average Cost per Message in Florins.
1851	44,911	128,736	2.86
1852	62,716	209,547	3.34
1853	109,347	308,159	2.81
1854	190,522	549,697	2.88
1855	204,221	607,745	2.97
1856	251,948	778,294	3.08
1857	381,720	888,905	2.32
1858	419,449	760,811	1.81
1859	692,379	951,240	1.37
1860	700,795	991,275	1.41
1861	846,953	1,226,404	1.44
1862	946,675	1,267,966	1.33
1863	1,130,625	1,290,447	1.14
1864	1,610,663	1,322,948	0.82
1865	1,786,955	1,435,478	0.80
1866	2,507,472	1,644,742	0.65

Austria transmitted 44,911 messages in 1851, and 381,720 in 1857, being an increase of over 800 per cent without any average reduction in rates. The increase in the number of messages from 1857 to 1866 was less than 700 per cent, notwithstanding the great reduction in the rates from 2.32 to 0.65 florins.

BELGIUM.

The statistics respecting the working of the telegraph in Belgium are used by Mr. Washburne primarily to prove the superior advantages and excellence of the Belgian telegraphic system and arrangement, but chiefly to show that a cheapened rate has increased its use, and that to secure that result in this country the telegraph must be placed under governmental control.

Scarcely any two nations could be named whose conditions are more unlike.

The area of Belgium is about one fourth that of the State of New York, with nearly the same population. Its greatest length is 175 miles, its width 105.

The three chief cities of Belgium are not more than thirty miles apart, while those of secondary rank are equally contiguous. All the railroads in the kingdom belong to the government, and a large proportion of the telegraph offices are at the railway stations, the post-offices being merely offices of deposit, from which messages are despatched free of charge to the nearest telegraph office, if in the same district; otherwise by special messenger, on the payment of an extra fee.

As the government of the United States owns no railroads, they could not use the stations for offices, except by special arrangements, which can as readily be effected by private companies.

TABLE D.

Statement showing the Progress of Telegraphy in Belgium.

DATE.	Number of Messages.	Gross Receipts in Francs.	Average Cost per Message in Francs.
1851	14,025	88,674	6.32
1852	27,217	165.973	6.07
1853	52,050	265,536	5.10
1854	60,415	280,845	4.65
1855	61,443	265,939	4.33
1856	99,273	359,579	3.62
1857	119,050	407,011	3.42
1858	145,726	413,926	2.83
1859	196,240	506,006	2.57
1860	225,819	527,743	2.34
1861	268,968	588,532	2.19
1862	291,787	605,044	2.07
1863	416,113	612,313	1.47
1864	564,497	789,399	1.44
1865	674,034	865,640	1.28
1866	1,128,005	962,213	0.85
1867	1,293,770	1,074,214	0.85

TABLE E.

Statement showing the Lengths of Lines, &c.

DATE.	Lengths of Lines.	Lengths of Wires.	Number of Stations.	Number of Instruments.
	Miles.	Miles.		
1862	1,174	2,983	196	290
1863	1,644	3,875	252	365
1864	1,856	4,421	280	420
1865	2,000	5,400	307	460
1866	2,187	6,146	356	556
1867	2,232	7,161	374	574

TABLE F.

Statement showing the Number of Messages.

DATE.	Inland.	International.	Transit.	Total.
1851	6,652	6,054	1,319	14,025
1852	9,807	10,103	7,307	27,217
1853	14,159	20,656	17,539	52,050
1854	16,719	29,492	14,204	60,415
1855	17,279	34,725	9,429	61,443
1856	32,862	45,375	21,036	99,273
1857	41,434	48,367	29,249	119,050
1858	47,673	58,094	39,959	145,726
1859	65,465	83,780	46,995	196,240
1860	80,216	95,499	50,404	225,819
1861	97,945	115,121	55,902	268,968
1862	105,274	129,935	56,578	291,787
1863	188,825	162,178	65,110	416,113
1864	252,301	197,547	96,649	546,497
1865	332,721	252,133	89,183	674,037
1866	692,536	306,596	128,873	1,128,005
1867	819,668	359,652	114,550	1,293,870

TABLE G.

Statement showing the Gross Receipts.

DATE.	Inland.	International.	Transit.	Total.
	Francs.	Francs.	Francs.	Francs.
1852.............................	....	....	....	88,674
1853.............................	....	....	....	265,536
1854.............................	....	....	....	280,845
1855.............................	....	....	....	265,939
1856.............................	....	....	....	359,579
1857.............................	....	....	....	407,011
1858.............................	....	....	....	413,926
1859.............................	....	....	....	506,006
1860.............................	142,344	232,877	149,969	527,743
1861.............................	171,225	237,748	158,558	588,532
1862.............................	176,643	280,449	147,952	605,044
1863.............................	211,063	277,266	124,033	612,368
1864.............................	282,591	307,956	198,850	789,399
1865.............................	345,289	340,103	180,247	865,640
1866.............................	408,634	369,900	183,680	962,214
1867.............................	480,887	444,245	149,082	1,074,214

TABLE H.

Statement showing the Receipts and Expenditure of Telegraphs.

DATE.	Receipts.	Expenditures.	Loss.	Profits.
	Francs.	Francs.	Francs.	Francs.
1851.....................	88,674	309,116	220,431.39	....
1852.....................	165,973	102,947	....	63,025.88
1853.....................	265,536	170,735	....	94,800.85
1854.....................	280,845	139,795	....	141,050.61
1855.....................	265,939	161,500	....	104,439.67
1856.....................	359,579	202,599	....	156,980.11
1857.....................	407,011	283,171	....	123,840.23
1858.....................	413,926	293,891	....	120,035.19
1859.....................	506,006	375,343	....	130,662.75
1860.....................	527,743	403,500	....	124,243.73
1861.....................	588,532	408,261	....	180,271.33
1862.....................	605,044	515,800	....	89,241.86
1863.....................	612,363	653,280	41,417.19	....
1864.....................	789,399	670,424	....	118,974.83
1865.....................	865,640	948,516	22,876.20	....
1866.....................	962,214	1,217,496	255,282.00	....
1867.....................	1,074,214	1,128,703	54,489.00	....

TABLE I.

Statement showing the Average of Receipts, reduced to Dollars, and the Average of Messages.

DATE.	Gross Receipts.		Number of Messages.				Number of Inhabitants averaging to each Station.
	Average per Mile of Line, in Gold.	Average per Station, in Gold.	Average per Station.		Average for each 1,000 inhabitants.		
			Inland.	Total.	Inland.	Total.	
1851....	....	....	....	....	....	....	....
1852....	....	....	....	....	....	....	....
1853....	....	....	....	....	....	....	....
1854....	....	....	....	....	....	....	....
1855....	....	....	....	....	....	....	....
1856....	....	....	....	....	....	....	....
1857....	....	....	....	....	....	....	....
1858....	....	....	....	....	11	24	....
1859....	....	....	....	....	15	34	....
1860....	....	....	....	....	18	40	....
1861....	....	....	....	....	22	48	....
1862....	$103.08	$616.37	537	1,488	23	52	23,980
1863....	74.50	586.00	749	1,651	41	78	17,857
1864....	85.06	563.85	901	1,951	56	100	16,071
1865....	86.56	563.94	1,084	2,195	74	130	14,658
1866....	87.89	540.00	1,945	3,168	150	217	12,690
1867....	91.70	666.40	2,191	3,450	....	....	....

The telegrams of Belgium are of three distinct sorts, — internal, international, and transit. The system differs essentially from that of the United States, inasmuch as the principal business of the Belgian telegraph is to transmit messages from one country to another, whilst the principal business of the American telegraph is the conveyance of internal messages. The only international messages transmitted on the lines in the United States are those sent to Europe by the Atlantic cable, to Cuba by the Cuban cable, and to the various stations in the Dominion of Canada.

One of the arguments used in favor of the assumption of telegraphs by government is, that in its hands the telegraph is more largely accessible to the people, and more freely used. The facts are as follows, giving Belgium the benefit of the increase of messages shown by the last reduction of her tariff.

BELGIUM.

Population, 5,000,000 ; messages, 692,586. Ratio, one message to each seventh person.

GREAT BRITAIN.

Population, 29,500,000 ; messages, 5,781,189. Ratio, one message to each fifth person.

UNITED STATES.

Population, 31,148,047 ; messages, 12,904,770. Ratio, one message to every two and one half persons.

These facts prove a clear advantage in favor of private control.

BAVARIA.

This country possesses 2,115 miles of lines, and 4,945 miles of wire.

Gross receipts for 1866, 322,886 florins. Expenditures, 258,625 florins.

DENMARK.

This country now contains 2,515 miles of wire, and eighty-nine telegraphic stations open to the public. The Morse apparatus is the only one employed. Of these eighty-nine stations, fifty-three belong to the government, twenty-one to private telegraph companies, and fifteen to railroads.

The tariff is fixed at ninety cents for a local telegram of twenty words between any points in the kingdom. In 1867 there were transmitted 308,150 telegrams, of which 174,560 were local and 133,590 foreign. All the stations send written despatches in all languages, even in cipher, the only conditions being legible writing in an alphabet transmissible by the Morse apparatus.

Money orders to the amount of 50 rix-dollars can be paid at all post-offices by means of the telegraph. The sum being deposited at the original office, an official telegram is sent to the place designated, ordering payment.

For this service the sender has only to pay the tariff on the official telegram. Messages can be sent from points where there are no telegraphic stations, by sending them by post or by any other mode of transportation to the nearest telegraph station. These telegrams can be paid by a postage-stamp affixed to a designated part of the form. These forms are the same as the printed envelopes, and can be procured at all post and telegraph offices. At the top of these forms is printed an extract from the rules for the transmission of despatches. The stamps are detached from the forms and sent to the Department of Finances at the same time that the other reports are forwarded. It is proposed to extend these privileges to the private and railroad telegraph stations.

From 1863 to 1867 the telegraphic intercourse between the Scandinavian countries has increased each year twenty-five per cent.

ENGLAND.

England was among the first countries in Europe to adopt the electric telegraph ; and, next to the United States, is the foremost nation in the world in the extent of her lines, the number of her offices, the cheapness of her rates, and the number of messages annually transmitted. With a population about three quarters as large as that of France, she possesses nearly twice as many telegraph stations, and annually transmits more than twice as many messages.

There are in operation in Europe fifty-five submarine cables, varying in length from three to 1,500 miles, and containing a total length of over 11,000 miles of insulated wire, nearly all of which were laid and are owned by English capitalists. The success of the Atlantic cables, also laid by English companies, is another illustration of what can be accomplished by private enterprise untrammelled by governmental interference ; and affords a striking contrast to the fate of the Red Sea cable laid by the British government, and which has proved one of the greatest failures recorded in the annals of submarine telegraphy. This cable, which was to connect Suez and Kurrachee, 3,500 miles in length, was laid in five sections, but never worked a day through its entire length.

For some unexplained reason the British post-office department has been determined to absorb the telegraph system of the United Kingdom, and through the indefatigable efforts of Mr. Scudamore, one of the secretaries of the department, the British government was finally induced to purchase the property of all the telegraph companies in the kingdom, and thus monopolize the business. The price to be paid for the lines is twenty times the net earnings of the companies for the past year.

That the English government has made a serious mistake in assuming the control of the telegraph we have no question; but its operation will be better in its hands than it would be in that of our government, for the reason that its employees are not removed with every change of administration, as government officials are in the United States.

Statement showing the Progress of Telegraphy in Great Britain and Ireland.

Year.	No. of Offices.	No. of Miles of Line.	No. of Miles of Wire.	No. of Messages.
1860	1,032	10,854	51,556	1,863,839
1861	1,391	11,538	55,004	2,123,589
1862	1,616	12,711	57,879	2,676,352
1863	1,755	13,944	65,726	3,186,724
1864	1,831	14,981	72,374	3,924,855
1865	2,040	16,066	77,440	4,662,687
1866	2,151	16,588	80,466	5,781,189

FRANCE.

The French system of telegraphs comprised, in 1866, 20,628 miles of route, 68,687 miles of wire, and 1,209 stations open to the public. The number of messages amounted to 2,842,554. The gross receipts for the year were 7,707,590, and the expenditures were 8,983,460, showing a loss for the year of 1,275,870.

The receipts are divided as follows: —

301	stations	collect	less than		200 francs each.
179	"	"	from	200 to 500	" "
185	"	"	"	500 to 1,000	" "
354	"	"	"	1,000 to 5,000	" "
84	"	"	"	5,000 to 10,000	" "
63	"	"	"	10,000 to 30,000	" "
17	"	"	"	30,000 to 50,000	" "
12	"	"	"	50,000 to 100,000	" "
6	"	"	"	100,000 to 200,000	" "
4	"	"	"	200,000 to 300,000	" "
2	"	"	"	300,000 to 400,000	" "
1	"	"		527,000.	
1	"	"		620,000.	

1,209 total.

These stations are situated in 89 departments, viz. : —

1. Départment de la Seine,   collecting 2,822,367 francs.
2.   "   Bouches de Rhone,   "   747,228   "
3.   "   Seine inférieure,   "   608,737   "
4.   "   Rhone,   "   348,514   "
5.   "   Nord,   "   265,705   "
6.   "   Gironde,   "   260,615   "
7.   "   Loire inférieure,   "   139,797   "
8.   "   Haut Rhin,   "   135,483   "
9.   "   Hérault,   "   134,388   "
10.   "   Alpes Maritimes,   "   **101,183**   "

Nine other departments collect annually between 90,000 **down to** 50,000 francs, **the remaining** seventy from 49,000 down **to 4,653** francs.

Paris (**Départment** de la Seine) has forty-six stations within the fortifications. The gross receipts amounted, in 1866, to 2,794,-768.40 francs, being more than one third of the **total** receipts of the whole empire.

The receipts **in Paris are divided as follows** : —

Place de la **Bourse,**   ·   **527,906** francs.
Rue de la Grenelle,   **283,972**   "
Grand Hotel,   271,880   "
Rue Lafayette,   250,967   "
Rue J. J. Rousseau,   198,465   "
Rue St. Cécile,   139,916   "
Aux Champs Elysées,   131,059   "

Six other stations collect from 85,000 to 50,000, six from 50,000 **to 20,000 ;** the remainder from 19,000 **down** to 2,123 francs.

The telegraph system of France constitutes a distinct department of the government service under Viscount **A.** de Vougy as Director-General. Under him are five general inspectors, forming a kind of council, nine division inspectors, seventy-five inspectors, thirty-eight sub-inspectors, and one electrical engineer. There are altogether 3,708 persons on the staff.

DECREES REGULATING THE USE OF THE TELEGRAPH IN FRANCE.

The following is a digest of the decrees issued by the French government regulating the use of the telegraph in the empire.

1st. All persons whose identity is established are allowed to correspond by the government electric telegraph.

2d. Private correspondence is always subordinate to the necessity of government service.

3d. Despatches are to be written in *ordinary and intelligible language*, dated and signed by the sender, and to be given to the officer of the telegraph station, whose duty it is to *copy in full the despatch*, with the address of the sender.

4th. The director of a station may, on grounds of public order and morality, *refuse to transmit a despatch.* In case of dispute, reference is to be made, in Paris, to the minister of the interior; in the provinces to the prefect, sub-prefect, or other constituted authority. On the receipt of a despatch, the director of the station may *withhold its delivery* for like reasons.

5th. Private correspondence may be suspended at any time by the government. *The government will not assume any responsibility for errors in the transmission of despatches.*

6th. The director of the station must be satisfied as to the identity of the sender's signature. If the director refuses the transmission of a message, he must state his reason in writing on the despatch. He must indorse on it "political," "offensive," "not consistent with public good," etc.

7th. No line of electric telegraph can be established or employed for the transmission of correspondence except by the government, or on its authority. *Any person transmitting, without authority, signals from one place to another, whether by electric telegraph, or in any other way, is liable to imprisonment from one month to a year, and a fine of 1,000 to 10,000 francs, and the government may order the destruction of the apparatus and telegraph employed.*

8th. Any one *accidentally* interrupting the correspondence of the electric telegraph, or injuring in any way the lines or apparatus, is liable to a fine of from 16 to 3,000 francs.

9th. Any one wilfully causing an interruption, by injuring the lines or apparatus, is punishable by imprisonment from three months to two years, and a fine of 100 to 1,000 francs. Any one who shall menace an operator during periods of insurrectionary movements is subject to a fine of 1,000 to 5,000 francs.

10th. Written statements by telegraph officers to be received as evidence in all complaints.

11th. Reimbursements of charges on despatches, in consequence of delays or errors in transmission, cannot be made except by the administration. When a despatch is withdrawn by the forwarder before transmission, the expense of delivery only can be refunded.

The charge on despatches sent in the night will be double the usual tariff for the day business (the exact opposite of the American rule).

PECULIAR CHARACTER OF THE FRENCH TELEGRAPH.

The telegraph lines in France are nearly all owned and managed by the government. The English Submarine Company, however, is a private enterprise, and works from Paris through Calais to the United Kingdom. There is also another company organized under permission of the imperial government, for the extension of the lines into the French colonies of Africa. This association is called the Mediterranean Electric Telegraph Company, and it has constructed its line from Spezzia, in Sardinia, across Corsica, Sardinia, and the Mediterranean, to Bóne, in Africa.

The telegraph in France is regarded as one of the most important arms of the government, and the wires are known as the *fingers of the police.* The Emperor would no sooner relinquish their control than he would that of his armies. By imperial decree, every operator is created a spy in the service of the government. The wires from every part of France centre in the imperial chamber, and not a message passes throughout the empire which is not examined by government inspectors.

Of the promptness, regularity, or correctness with which French telegraphs are conducted no proof is given by which superior excellence is established. There is nothing in the whole exhibit, or in the actual working of the French telegraphs, which presents any reason for the assumption that governments manage telegraphs better than the people.

TABLE J.

Statement showing the Progress of Telegraphy in France.

Date.	Number of Messages.	Gross Receipts in Francs.	Average Cost per Message in Francs.
1851...............................	9,014	76,722	7.84
1852...............................	48,105	542,891	11.28
1853...............................	142,061	1,511,909	10.64
1854...............................	236,018	2,064,983	8.74
1855...............................	254,532	2,487,159	9.77
1856...............................	360,299	3,191.102	8.68
1857...............................	412,616	3,333,695	8.06
1858...............................	463,973	3,516,633	7.60
1859...............................	598,701	4,022,799	6.72
1860...............................	720,250	4,188 065	5.81
1861...............................	920,357	4,919,737	5.34
1862...............................	1,518,044	5,302,440	3.49
1863...............................	1,754,867	5,937,904	3.38
1864...............................	1,967,748	6,123,272	3.13
1865..	2,473,747	7,052,139	2.88
1866...............................	2,842,554	7,707,590	2.79

INCREASE IN TELEGRAMS NOT DUE TO LOW RATES.

It will be observed, by an examination of the above table, that low tariffs are not the only causes of the enlarged use of the telegraph. The annual percentage of increase in messages, as tariffs were gradually reduced, was vastly less than during those years when the rates remained unchanged. During the year of 1851 only 9,014 telegrams were transmitted through the French empire, the tariff averaging $1.60 per message. Five years later, notwithstanding that the average cost per message had been *increased* to $1.73, the number of messages had increased to 360,299, and in 1858 to 463,973, — more than fifty times the number sent in 1851, or *an increase of more than five thousand per cent in eight years, without any reduction in rates.* The increase in the number of messages during the next eight years, from 1858 to 1866, was only six hundred per cent, notwithstanding a reduction in the tariff from 7.60 to 2.79 francs.

This same peculiarity of increase, without regard to the cost, is also observable in all other countries, as will be seen by a perusal of the official tables.

TABLE K.

Statement showing the Progress of Telegraphy in France.

Date.	Number of Messages Annually.			Gross Receipts per Annum in Francs.			Average Cost per Message.		
	Home.	Foreign.	Total.	Home.	Foreign.	Total.	Home.	Foreign.	Total.
				Fr. ct.	Fr. ct.	Fr. ct.	Fr. ct.	Fr. ct.	Fr. ct.
1851			9,014			76,722.60			7.84
1852			48,195			542,891.58			11.28
1853			142,061			1,511,909.57			10.64
1854			233,018			2,064,983.71			8.84
1855			254,582			2,487,159.21			9.77
1856			330,299			3,191,102.04			8.68
1857			413,616			3,333,695.74			8.06
1858	349,887	114,086	463,973	1,749,913.35	1,721,715.35	3,516,633.70	5.13	15.09	7.60
1859	453,998	144,703	598,701	2,072,314.15	1,950,485.63	4,022,799.78	4.57	13.48	6.72
1860	568,395	151,885	720,250	2,338,525.21	1,829,540.05	4,188,065.26	4.15	12.06	5.81
1861	734,252	186,357	920,357	2,840,445.84	2,079,292.12	4,919,737.86	3.82	11.16	5.34
1862	1,291,774	226,270	1,518,044	2,934,490.21	2,317,950.34	5,302,440.55	2.31	10.24	3.49
1863	1,490,023	264,844	1,754,867	3,305,993.85	2,631,911.08	5,937,904.93	2.22	9.94	3.38
1864	1,654,406	313,342	1,937,748	3,565,933.68	2,557,338.38	6,123,272.06	2.15	8.16	3.13
1865	2,098,645	375,102	2,473,747	4,159,445.45	2,892,694.34	7,052,139.79	1.93	7.71	2.88
1866	2,379,681	462,873	2,842,554	4,513,095.32	3,194,495.29	7,707,590.61	1.90	6.90	2.79

GREECE.

The Kingdom of Greece has twelve telegraph stations. All the messages between the Greek and European lines pass through Turkey, and consequently the rate is very high. It is proposed to establish a direct line between Greece and Southern Italy by continuing the Corfu cable to Pauras or Missolonghi, across the Ionian Islands.

PRUSSIA.

In Prussia the number of messages transmitted in 1866, the last year of which we have data, was 1,964,030, and the gross receipts were 1,275,785 thalers, making the average cost per message seventy cents in our currency. Prussia had in that year a population of 17,740,000, and the area of her territory was somewhat less than the New England States and New York. Distance being regarded, the Prussian rates were at that period double our own.

TABLE L.

Statement showing the Progress of Telegraphy in Prussia.

Date.	Number of Messages.	Gross Receipts in Thalers.	Average Cost per Message in Thalers.
1852	48,751	114,539	2.350
1853	85,161	209,944	2.460
1854	116,313	328,506	2.820
1855	152,820	434,122	2.840
1856	221,411	591,038	2.670
1857	241,545	726,517	3.010
1858	247,202	730,584	2.950
1859	349,997	808,521	2.310
1860	384,335	791,101	2.060
1861	459,002	875,783	1.988
1862	660,501	954,550	1.450
1863	877,583	1,039,961	1.180
1864	1,259,590	1,150,008	0.913
1865	1,527,455	1,242,489	0.812
1866	1,964,030	1,275,785	0.656

It will be observed that the number of messages transmitted in 1852 was 48,751, and in 1860, 384,335, being an increase in nine years of nearly 800 per cent, although there was no reduction in the average tariff during this period. From 1860 to 1866 there was an increase of only 500 per cent, notwithstanding a reduction in the rates from 2.06 to 0.656 thalers per message.

Prussia was among the earliest of Continental countries to adopt the electric telegraph, and it is still far in advance of most of its neighbors in the practical development of the enterprise; and yet, with a population more than half as great as the United States, she only transmits one sixth as many messages per annum. Were the system left to private enterprise, as in this country, there can be no doubt that this enlightened and thrifty people would greatly extend the system, and in place of the meagre supply of 538 offices she would have upwards of 2,000, and in place of 1,964,030 messages per annum would transmit seven or eight millions.

RUSSIA.

European Russia, with a population considerably more than twice as great as the United States, contains but 308 offices, or one to

230,000 of people; and sends annually but 838,653 messages, or one to each 80,723 of her population.

Any person examining the telegraphic map of Russia will be satisfied that the rose-colored descriptions of government telegraphs as illustrated in Russia are overdrawn. The lines radiating from St. Petersburg, and extending to Warsaw, Moscow, Odessa, Sebastopol, Nichni-Novgorod, to the Persian frontier, and to Kiakhta in Siberia, — all important military points, — and with scarcely any connecting interior lines, suggest anything but a desire to afford ample telegraphic facilities to the people.

SWITZERLAND.

The situation of Switzerland, in the centre of Europe, and forming the pathway between nations, places her in a peculiar position with reference to the transmission of messages from one country to another. Just as Belgium is situated in relation to intercourse between France and Germany, so Switzerland is placed in regard to telegraphic communication between France and Italy, and Italy and Germany. Switzerland, from many circumstances, is a country in which telegraphic communication is eminently useful. In the first place it is a mountainous country, over which postal communication is necessarily slow, and conducted at all seasons under disadvantages. Besides all this, Switzerland, at certain seasons of the year, is a country full of travellers and tourists from all parts of the world, who find great advantage and convenience in being able to transmit short messages from one place to another, respecting hotel accommodations, baggage arrangements, lost packages, horses, places in the diligence, and general matters relating to their route, as well as business and social messages to their relatives, friends, and agents at home.

Switzerland is in the same position with Belgium in respect to the means of cheap telegraphic communication. The railways of the country all belong to the state; so that every railway is available, without charge, for the passage of wires along the line, and every railway official may be employed for telegraphic service, at the pleasure of the government, for nothing. It is scarcely necessary to point out how different must be the working of such a system from that of the United States, where the railways are in the hands of private companies, and with whom terms have to be made for the right of way.

NO ANALOGY BETWEEN THE UNITED STATES AND SWITZERLAND.

The analogy between the United States and Switzerland seems in every sense imperfect. The telegraph stations in Switzerland only number 252, or less than the number contained within a radius of fifty miles in and around the city of New York.

The total number of despatches transmitted annually in and through Switzerland only amounted in 1866 to 668,916, whilst of these probably more than half were either transit or international. These transit telegrams, of which there are none in our country, involve a most important difference. Belgium and Switzerland can make up the deficiencies which arise from losses on internal communication by the surplus derived from transit telegrams.

In 1852 the average number of messages per day, for all Switzerland, was less than ten. As the system became extended, and the people were educated to its use, the number of messages increased, until in 1866 they exceeded 2,000 per day, approximating, for the entire country, the number sent and received daily by fifteen female operators in one of the rooms of the Western Union Telegraph Company, in the city of New York. Probably one half of these were transit messages passing through Switzerland from stations in France, Belgium, and Italy, leaving about 1,000 messages per day of inland business, which, divided among 252 offices, would leave an average of a little less than *four messages per day for each office!* This is not a very magnificent result, and is not over encouraging as a model system, which gives to its twenty-five cantons ten offices, with an average revenue from each; for inland business, of only three francs per day! And this, notwithstanding that the government coaches convey, without any extra charge, messages, from towns unsupplied with offices, to the nearest telegraph station.

TABLE M.

Statement showing the Progress of Telegraphy in Switzerland.

DATE.	Number of Messages.	Gross Receipts in Francs.	Average Cost per Message in Francs.
1852	2,876	3,541.95	
1853	82,586	127,870.04	1.55
1854	129,167	208,887.36	1.62
1855	162,851	251,391.27	1.53
1856	227,072	319,947.22	1.44
1857	260,164	369,226.01	1.42
1858	247,102	343,597.38	1.35
1859	286,876	425,587.57	1.48
1860	303,930	408,429.04	1.34
1861	331,933	448,056.05	1.35
1862	373,452	530,417.50	1.42
1863	456,871	630,748.26	1.38
1864	514,952	615,317.00	1.20
1865	591,214	726,564.16	1.23
1866	668,916	684,319.83	1.03
1867	708,974	775,024.00	1.09

It will be observed that the increase in the number of messages transmitted in Switzerland was from 2,876 in 1852 to 668,916 in 1866, or more than 230,000 per cent in fourteen years, although the tariff had only been reduced 33 per cent.

SPAIN.

Spain, with a population of over 16,000,000 souls, and possessing the advantages of forming the pathway between France and her African possessions, as well as between Portugal and the rest of Europe, transmits a less number of telegrams per annum than the Dominion of Canada, with her 3,000,000 inhabitants. That this insignificant amount of business for so great a country is owing to government control is evident from the following royal decree, issued in conformity with the request of the Minister of State, who says: "The petitions presented to your Majesty from different towns, companies, and private individuals are so numerous and repeated, praying that the advantages of telegraphic communications should be granted to them, that the minister who now humbly addresses your Majesty has lamented more than once that the care of the government has not extended that satisfaction to legitimate wishes so deserving of attention."

ROYAL DECREE RELATING TO TELEGRAPHS IN SPAIN.

In conformity with what the Minister of State for Home Affairs has proposed to me, for the concession of telegraph lines and stations.

I have decreed as follows : —

The districts, towns, and public establishments, who wish to form new lines or stations, *can solicit them from the government*, which will inquire into the influence of the establishment of the said lines or stations upon the state telegraphic system.

The necessary cost of the lines and service must be paid by the petitioners, and they must also give sufficient guaranty for the cost of repairs and service.

The petitioners will be obliged to pay to the state the difference that may result between the annual income and the cost of the service.

If at the expiration of five years the expenses exceed the returns, the line or station will be considered as property of the state. No line or station can be formed without the consent of the ministers in council.

Service in all kinds of stations and lines can only be performed by a staff from the government telegraph corps.

All despatches passing through Spain (including the Balearic Islands) and France (including Corsica) will pay the rate of five francs per message of 20 words, no matter from what telegraph office they proceed or to what station they are addressed. Each ten words or part of ten words, beyond 20, will pay half the amount of a single message.

The cost of a single message transmitted from France to Algeria, or *vice versa*, passing through the Spanish or submarine lines, as also of the messages between Spain and Algeria, transmitted either by land or French cables, will always be eight francs. The messages received or forwarded to Tunis will pay two francs more.

The messages exceeding 20 words will pay an extra charge, in accordance with the rule already established.

No despatch whatever will be delivered out of the radius of the locality wherein the station addressed to is situated, through any other means than by post.

Telegrams addressed to localities where there is no station will be delivered by the last telegraphic office to the post, which will undertake to convey them to their destination as certified parcels.

When one despatch is addressed to several persons in the same locality, as many telegrams will be **charged** for as there are individuals to receive it.

The acknowledgment of the **receipt of a telegram** will be charged for as a new despatch.

Prepayment of despatches can be made, but if **no** *answer is returned, or if it should contain less words than those paid* **for,** *no return of any kind will* **be made.** If the answer contains more words than paid **for, the station which sends it** will charge the difference **between the amount paid and the** corresponding one **to this new despatch.**

The claims for delay or irregularity of telegrams will only give **occasion for** future inquiry into the causes which have produced **the irregularity** in the service, for the knowledge of the interested party, **and** to punish the functionary who should **prove** to be culpable.

Given at Aranjuez, on the 22d **May, 1864.**

If there is any special **benefit** accruing to the people of **Spain** by having the telegraph **under** government control, we fail **to** discover it.

TURKEY.

Turkey **contains** twenty-eight telegraph stations, **of** which twelve are **open for night service,** nine during the whole of the day, **and** sev**e**n **for** a part only. Constantinople has two stations open for international correspondence, — one at Stamboul, the other at Pera; the first is principally confined to the transmission of messages for the Ottoman government, and the second for that of ambassadors and private persons. In the case of an interruption of the cable which crosses the Hellespont, the Dardanelles station is removed to Ķaled-Bahas, and the despatches are subjected **to an additional rate of 90** cents for their conveyance, by boat, **from Ķaled-Bahas to** the Dardanelles. The tariff, upon messages between Paris **to any Turkish** station, varies from $ 2.80 to $ 6.00, **according** to the distance.

The construction of lines in Turkey is of the most defective description, and the materials used very inferior. The lines pass over the steepest and most inaccessible hills; and this state of things is made worse by a very inadequate inspection, by men who are both too few in number, wretchedly paid, and generally incompetent. Repairers are compelled to provide and keep a horse out of their pay of 300 piastres ($13.04) per month. The chiefs of stations, and all other employees, are Turks, whose lazy habits and incompetency cannot be wondered at, when the smallness of their pay is considered. Added to these difficulties, the service has to endure very frequent and arbitrary occupation of the wires by the government, interrupting, on many occasions, business of the most pressing nature, for the transmission of some trivial communication, which would lose nothing by a short delay. It may be imagined that as the service is in the hands of government, much depends upon the director-general of the department. Unfortunately, this official is in the unenviable position of holding office on such a poor tenure that it may be said he has a daily apprehension of being turned out, and replaced by one of those numerous intriguers who swarm about the cabinets of the ministers, or work through the more effectual influence of the harem, — the great bane of the country. It has been proposed to the Turkish government to employ a large staff of English inspectors and operators, but the natural jealousy of employing foreigners stands in the way. The Turks insist upon having all messages sent through in Turkish, so that frequently, when re-translated, they bear very slight resemblance to the original.

All the important telegraphic intercourse between Europe and India passes through the Turkish dominions. The effect of the control of the Turkish government over the telegraph is most disastrous, and renders this important connection with India almost worthless.

Repeated efforts have been made by the English telegraph companies, who have so great an interest in the successful operation of these lines, to induce the Turkish government to relinquish its management of them, but thus far without success.

REASONS

GOVERNMENT SHOULD NOT ENTER INTO COMPETITION WITH THE PEOPLE IN THE OPERATION OF THE TELEGRAPH.

THE foregoing presentation of facts has shown that there are no sufficient grounds for destroying the value of the investments of the people in existing telegraph companies by governmental competition, the telegraph system of this country being unrivalled in its extent, unequalled in its administration, and unparalleled for the low rates which it has always maintained.

In this country the people have not been accustomed to rely upon the government to provide those things for them which they are able to secure by their own exertions. If this principle is right in regard to one enterprise, it is also in relation to all others; and if infringed upon in the case of the telegraph companies, what pursuit will be safe from governmental interference?

It is undoubtedly true that, were tariffs designed simply to provide a revenue to support the lines, they are capable of reduction, provided present arrangements with railroad companies and others could be maintained, by which the labor of the one is utilized in the service of the other. But for this the country makes no demand. It recognizes the telegraph as a legitimate enterprise for the investment of the capital and labor of its citizens. If false counsels guide its development, public reprobation is ready with its remedy. Its absorption by government would not only be a public calamity, but a breach of the theory and spirit of our institutions, and would soon result in its necessary return to individual control.

POLITICAL REASONS WHY GOVERNMENT SHOULD NOT CONTROL THE TELEGRAPH.

One of the most serious objections to the government of the United States assuming the control of the telegraph is the political

one. In monarchical countries, where the sovereignty is a patri-
mony of a particular family, and where no change is made except
by revolution, everything which tends towards the permanence of
the reigning dynasty is looked upon as in the interest of law and
order, and for these reasons the absorption of the telegraphs by
the government is regarded as a proper and legitimate act, and
consistent with the public weal ; but in a republic, where the
rulers are changed periodically, and where the purity of the elec-
tions is of the first importance, the placing of so great a power
in the hands of the government would be a public calamity. It
might be supposed that rulers could be elected who would not take
advantage of the control of the telegraph for selfish purposes, but
the temptation to do so would be great, and, even if not yielded
to, the suspicions of the people would be constantly aroused, and
confidence in its impartial administration would be destroyed. In
every election the whole army of postmasters and the machinery
of the department is enlisted in the service of the party in power.
Shall we give it the telegraph also ? What would be the influence
on election returns ?

The censorship of telegraphic correspondence, always a subject
of public disapprobation, is generally exercised by all governments
which have its management. In France the control of the telegraph by government is loudly complained of, in consequence of
notorious abuses which result from it. Amongst other things, it is
well known that the authorities of the Bourse, in Paris, have opportunities of seeing every telegram which reaches or leaves that
city on matters relating to the stock exchange operations.

THE POST-OFFICE DEPARTMENT NOT COMPETENT TO MANAGE THE TELEGRAPHS.

If it should ever appear to be for the public good that this agency,
so capable of use as a political power, should pass into the hands of
government, it seems proper to await such a demonstration of the
self-sustaining capacity of the department under whose control it
is proposed to be placed, and such efficiency in that service, as
will furnish reasonable assurance of ability for the united control
without burden to the state, or lessened convenience to the people.
A department which is still confessedly imperfect, which can-

not even **tell the number of letters which it transmits per an-num,** whose receipts are unequal to the cost of service by over $6,000,000,* which could not secure skilled labor in this new field except by foraging from existing enterprises, and which could not avoid heavy losses at the rates proposed, is not at present a fit recipient of so important a trust.

The Post-Office Department, which already has more duties than it is able to perform, instead of seeking to absorb the telegraphs, had better apply itself to its proper task of developing the correspondence of the country, and **endeavor to make** itself financially profitable to the nation, instead of a serious burden.

That the post-office undertakes **more** than **it can** perform is shown by the delays and irregularities of the **service,** and the enormous **and constantly** increasing number of its dead letters, **which amounted,** in 1867, to over 4,500,000 ! Were the telegraph companies to deal with the messages committed to them for transmission as the post-office deals with the letters committed to its care, there would be good grounds for governmental interference ; but **there are very few complaints of non-delivery of telegrams.**

It should be borne in mind that electric telegraphy **is a science, and** its successful operation **requires a** thorough knowledge of electricity, skill in manipulating the apparatus, and many years of constant training in the practical duties of the business. Many of the employees of this company have been constantly in the service for more than a score of years, and still consider themselves students in this **new field of practical science :** without wishing to be invidious in our comparisons, we may fairly say that the intelligence and skill **which are** ample for **the duties of** filling a bag with letters and despatching them by horse or steam power, would not be competent to the **duties** of successfully transmitting **an** important despatch through the invisible agency of the electric current.

GOVERNMENT ASSUMES NO RESPONSIBILITY.

Another serious drawback to the **value** of the telegraph under government management is **its failure to make** reparation to pri-

---

* The postal revenue for the year ending June 30th, 1868, was $16,292,600.80, and the expenditures during the same period $22,730,592.65, showing an excess of expenditures of $6,337,991.85. From the report of the Postmaster-General.

vate individuals for losses caused by the errors or imperfection of its service. In no country where the telegraph exists under government control is there any assumption of accountability for errors or delays in the transmission of messages. In some countries they will not even inquire into the cause of delay or errors, and in others, as in Spain, they will only do so for the purpose of punishing the delinquent employee, but in no case to reimburse the patron of the telegraph for his loss. This failure to assume any responsibility in the matter is of great importance to the public. The amount paid by the Western Union Telegraph Company per annum, on account of these unavoidable errors and delays, is very considerable. The public would be reluctant to leave the correct transmission and delivery of their important messages to the chances of a government system which is notoriously defective, and which would in no case reimburse them for losses occasioned by errors in the transmission of their telegrams, or failure to send them at all. The scheme proposed by Mr. Hubbard, owing to the divided responsibility of the service, would be even worse than the absorption of the lines by the government. Public opinion could not reach the contractor, because he is the servant of the government, and not of the public, and it would fail to influence the Post-Office Department, as it does not itself perform the service, and, because being a department, it is practically irresponsible. How much influence, for example, has public opinion on the collectors of internal revenue or customs, or even the postmasters of this country?

If despatches were left at the post-offices, or dropped in the street boxes, as provided for in Mr. Hubbard's bill, they would have to take their chances of transmission and delivery, with no recourse, in case of failure, for redress from any source. If a despatch should fail to reach its destination, and complaint was made to the postmaster, he would reply that he was not responsible for its transmission, and would refer the aggrieved person to the telegraph contractor; while the latter would answer that he was a servant of the government, and not responsible to the public for the imperfections of his service. And the result would be, that while the sender of the despatch obtained no redress, he would not have even the satisfaction of knowing which service was at fault, the post-office or the telegraph.

THE PROPOSITION TO ERECT COMPETITIVE GOVERNMENTAL TELEGRAPHS UNFOUNDED IN PUBLIC NECESSITY, UNJUST AND DELUSIVE.

The proposition to erect a competitive governmental telegraph line between Washington and New York, as described in the paper of Mr. Washburne, and the bill designed to authorize it, is a scheme founded upon no public necessity, unjust and delusive.

It is easily demonstrable that the tariff proposed by the bill, if adopted by the government, could only be maintained by large drafts upon the national treasury. It is well known that the active hours of telegraph service are about five, and the ordinary average of transmission not over fifty messages per hour, the general allowance being forty. Thus each of the four wires proposed to be erected under the bill would be capable of earning, at the maximum, five dollars per hour, or a total daily income of one hundred dollars, an amount unequal to the provision of the most ordinary indoor service, to say nothing of the cost of management, repairs of lines, battery power, stationery, and many other necessary expenses. The annual cost to our company of repairs and inspection on this route alone is $20,000.

This company denies the exorbitance of the rates it has adopted, and which it is now actively engaged in modifying so as to secure the fairest correspondence to other branches of labor, and the utmost development of the system. It therefore deprecates as illusory, as well as unjust, the proposal to establish rates lower than those which in Belgium have caused a loss of one third of the tariff on each message sent, and which, under the management of a department now showing an enormous annual deficit, cannot fail to prove perplexing and disastrous. It deprecates also, as utterly illusory, the idea that under such tariffs a product would be realized that would provide for the extension of the government lines to other regions. This delusion, which makes it possible for an intelligent public man to predicate so absurd a result, has for a basis that which is ever used to allure men into schemes of promised wealth. The insane speculation which, thirty years ago, ruined tens of thousands of our people, by counting the leaves of the *Morus multicaulis* as the products of veritable mulberry-trees, on which delighted caterpillars would feed, and enrich their owners with untold webs of native silk, was not more illusory than that which to-day, by showing the possibilities of each hour by day and night, crams the wires with possible messages which will never be sent, and estimates balances which cannot be earned.

This scheme would be unjust to government, by undermining and perilling a business which pays $300,000 per annum to its revenues, besides casting upon a nation, great because of the energy which has characterized its private enterprises, the odium of initiating competition with one of the most useful products of the national brain, before time has been given to complete the design of those who direct it, and to fully illustrate its capacity.

The policy and practice of the Western Union Telegraph Company favor a reduction of the rates on despatches as rapidly as the necessary expenses of the service will admit; *and if the government will abolish its tax on the receipts for transmitting telegrams, this company will immediately lower its rates until the reduction upon the gross amount of business done shall be twice as much as the tax remitted.*

This would lessen the rates for telegraphing nearly ten per cent, and would be a far better plan for furnishing cheaper telegraphic facilities to the people than the construction and operation of government lines at the expense of the national treasury.

THE TELEGRAPH BILL PROPOSED TO BE ENACTED BY CONGRESS WITHOUT NATIONAL EXAMPLE.

It must be borne in mind that the remunerativeness of telegraph lines depends largely upon the revenues of a few important cities, without which the enterprise would not have an income sufficient to support it. To take away the receipts of New York, Philadelphia, Baltimore, and Washington, with Boston, Chicago, Cincinnati, St. Louis, and a few others of like importance, would make it impossible for any company to maintain itself, far less to meet the constant demand of an enlarging population and new settlements for the extension of its lines. This is not peculiar to America. In Great Britain, where there are 2,151 stations, seventy-six per cent of the entire receipts are received at 18 stations, fifteen per cent at 81 stations, and only nine per cent at the residue. Even of the seventy-six per cent received at the 18 stations, one half of that whole percentage was received in London, and one quarter from two other cities.

In France, three departments collect 4,178,332, out of a total of 7,707,590 francs per annum ; and of this amount, Paris (Départment de la Seine) collects 2,794,768.40 francs, being more than one third of the total receipts of the whole empire.

The Western Union Telegraph Company's revenues come to it in a similar manner. From its 3,331 offices it derives its receipts as follows : —

From	136 offices,	.	.	.	75 per cent.
"	3195 "		.	.	25 per cent.

Of these 136 offices, a large proportion of their receipts is derived from twelve chief cities, of which four are on the route proposed by this bill.

Government, by thus operating lines of telegraph over the choicest and most productive route, at rates below the cost of the service, and which could only be maintained by large drafts upon the national treasury, would assume an attitude towards private telegraph enterprises of the most unjust and unexampled hostility.

Such a partial experiment as that proposed by Mr. Washburne, or even by Mr. Hubbard, would destroy the unitary character of the service which the Western Union Telegraph Company has done so much to secure, and would be a most decidedly reactionary measure.

Mr. Hubbard's bill to incorporate the United States Postal Telegraph Company, and to establish a postal-telegraph system, provides for the establishment of telegraph lines to all cities and villages of five thousand inhabitants and over in the United States. Were this scheme to be adopted, and the government thus enter into a partnership with the new company in the telegraph business, in accordance with the terms of this bill, what is to become of the smaller towns ? According to the census of 1860 there are only three hundred and thirteen cities and villages in the United States having the five thousand inhabitants necessary to entitle them to an office under this postal system. Who, then, is to maintain telegraphic facilities at the remaining three thousand eight hundred and thirteen small towns now having offices ?

Private companies, if driven out of the field by the establishment of this semi-government competing line, could not do it, and, as this scheme makes no provision for them, they must necessarily be deprived of the facilities they now enjoy. Under this bill Arkansas, Florida, and Oregon would not be entitled to an office; Minnesota, Mississippi, and South Carolina to but one; North Carolina, Texas, and Vermont to but two each; Delaware and Tennessee to but three; Connecticut, Georgia, Kentucky, and Michigan to but four; and Indiana, Kansas, Louisiana, Maine, Missouri, New Hampshire, Rhode Island, Virginia, and Wisconsin would be entitled to less than ten each, while those provided for the whole United States would be less in number than the branch offices furnished for the convenience of the public by the Western Union Telegraph Company at the hotels, docks, piers, and other places in the large towns alone.*

The proposal presented to Congress is one which the governments of Europe, from which it professes to draw its inspiration, have never entertained. No government there has ever yet attempted to engage in any public work by the destruction of the property of its people, except after just compensation. The recent example of Great Britain in acquiring the British lines of telegraph is eminently illustrative of this national justice. Neither cavilling with the nature or condition of their structure, cheapening the value of their property, nor defaming the officers of any company, the British Parliament doubles the valuation of its owners, and pays a price therefor which satisfies the most exacting. In striking contrast to this is the enterprise proposed to the American Congress by the Washburne bill, which begins by attacking the integrity of the official management of the existing system, depreciating the value of its property, and proposing the competitive use of a grand invention which it refused to purchase, and now proposes, without consideration, to possess. In such a project there is no national example which would give it sanction or respectability, even though, in times of great national peril, and amid the necessities of despotic governments, monarchs have at times seized and made their own the profitable traffic and pursuits of the people.

---

* The Postmaster-General is permitted to establish postal-telegraph stations at any city or village through which the lines of the contracting party may be extended, though said city or village contain less than five thousand inhabitants; but as the proposed company makes no provision for the payment of the operators or any of the expenses of such offices, while it secures to itself the receipts for telegrams, it is hardly to be expected that the Postmaster-General would feel disposed to open many stations under such circumstances.

APPENDIX.

APPENDIX.

THE TELEGRAPH AND THE GOVERNMENT.*

THE building of telegraph lines in the United States, from the date of their inauguration down to the present time, has been overdone. There are now too many wires for the business, at the prices that are charged; consequently there are few, if any, lines that pay a fair interest on the cost of their construction. So great is the cost of maintaining and operating lines, too, that it is a question whether sufficient business could be done, as it is conducted at very low rates, to pay expenses. In business hours, for example, there is a great rush of messages, — say from 9 A. M. to 3 P. M. — that is, between commercial centres. After 3 o'clock there is comparatively little business, except what is furnished by the newspapers. Consequently, in the after part of the day, and during the night, many wires and operators are idle. In order to make business for this portion of the twenty-four hours, the telegraph companies adopted a low schedule of rates for night messages, but this has been attended with poor success. The lines are mainly used, it is found, by business men and newspapers. Business messages require immediate delivery, and are not valuable except when transmitted and delivered during business hours. Hence the reduced rates for night messages has not created much new business. Neither would low rates for day messages create new business, unless the despatches could be promptly forwarded and delivered. Low rates for day messages, prompt delivery being insured, would undoubtedly largely increase the business, but this would require more wires and more men. The question then is, would the income at low rates be sufficient to pay for the increased expenditures? Telegraph managers have decided this question in the negative. There is, it must be borne in mind, a limit to the capacity of telegraph wires for conveying news. Herein this system differs from the postal system. There is, practically, no limit to the capacity of the railroad companies for carrying the mails, and, of course, the profits of the postal department are in proportion to the amount of business they transact. These preliminary remarks are made in order that the public may the better understand the proposition which has been made, and is being agitated, looking to the purchase of the telegraph lines by the government, and their operation in connection with the postal system. The pretext is, that the government could afford to reduce the tariff to a low point, say one cent per word for five hundred miles or less, and two cents for over five hundred up to one thousand, &c. This would make the tariff between Cincinnati and New York three cents, whereas it is now ten cents, for private messages. This is the pre-

* From the Cincinnati Gazette.

text, but the real secret of the movement is this. There are two parties who favor the proposition. One of these has been quietly buying up telegraph stock at thirty or forty cents on the dollar. They propose to have Congress pass a law authorizing the President to appoint three commissioners to value the telegraph lines of the United States and providing for their purchase at such valuation. Here is a fine chance for speculation. It would afford an admirable opening for the gentlemen who practise in the lobby. The second party favoring the purchase is composed of members of Congress who are anxious to have the franking privilege extended to the telegraph lines. What a splendid thing it would be if members of Congress could use the telegraph lines free, as they use the mails. But the people would have to pay for the free business on the telegraph lines, — pay dearly, too, as they pay for the uses and abuses of the postal franking privilege. Besides, the government, in connection with the postal system, is mainly conspicuous for its mismanagement. It does not compete successfully with private enterprise, and never can so long as the abominable system of filling and vacating offices is continued. The telegraph business is decidedly complicated. It requires skilful men to operate it. How would it be if telegraph offices were to be filled as post-offices and revenue offices are filled? We need not stop to answer this question. Besides, secrecy is an important feature of the telegraph business. It is not as carefully enforced as it should be; but what a political machine the telegraph would become if partisan politicians should get hold of it! Imagine the telegraph during an exciting presidential campaign, with one party controlling the wires and reading all the private despatches that passed over the lines! There would be no secrecy about it; neither would it be reliable, and in the end it would cost the people more than those using it would save. Not one man in twenty would use the telegraph if rates were even lower than is proposed; and consequently nineteen men would be taxed for the benefit of one. The whole thing would be a tax upon the people, without compensating advantages. If private enterprise, with sharp competition, cannot carry messages between New York and Cincinnati, at ten cents per word, and make money, the government could not do it at three cents, or at any price up to ten. Nothing more certain than that. Besides, the corruption connected with office-holding and office-getting, in this country, is sufficient to cause the people to shudder at the mere proposition to add fifty thousand offices to the already enormous federal patronage. The government is staggering now under the tremendous load of corruption consequent upon the federal patronage and the mode of distributing it, and the people must soon choose between a reform in this or a revolution. Let it be first demonstrated, therefore, that the government can successfully, honestly, and economically manage the business intrusted to it before it undertakes to assume exclusive control of other branches of private enterprise. But, as already stated, the present movement is merely a scheme to saddle upon the government the non-paying telegraph lines of the United States, at three or four times their value. The result would be amazing corruption in the management of the lines, the violation of private confidence for personal or political purposes, and a cost to the people for telegraphing greater than is now borne by those who use the wires.

POSTAL TELEGRAPH.—EXTENSION OF THE INTERFERENCE THEORY.*

WE beg the advocates of the **Postal** Telegraph scheme not to **stop.** The justification of what they propose **to** do, if in accordance with **their** theories of government, will cover many other things necessary to **be** done. After having taken possession of the telegraph lines, and increased the number of officers necessary to insure the harmonious working of their plan, let them turn their attention to the Express **business** of the country, in which there is room for **great** reform. This, we **are** told, is practically a monopoly, by the greed **of which the** transmission **of** merchandise and valuables from **one part of the country to another is** often slow, and always expensive. **If it is the province of the government** to take charge of the telegraphic **correspondence of the people, surely** there is no abuse of authority in undertaking **to carry, and in making** a monopoly of carrying, their **express** packages **; and the reasons which** commend this telegraph **scheme cover** and justify the extension of governmental interference **with the small** freight that the express lines usually convey. We state **these reasons** *seriatim,* just as the advocates of governmental telegraphing **rehearse** them. They are, first, cheapness; second, certainty; third, celerity; fourth, promotion of intercourse and traffic between different sections **of** the country; and consequently, **fifth,** the wider dissemination of intelligence. If **these are** sufficient,—**and no** promoter of the telegraph scheme **can** doubt **that they are,**—**they admit** of still wider application. Most of **the** telegraphic **correspondence of the** country is of a business character, and **so most** of the **service rendered** by the express is of the same sort. The telegraph and the **express are** the adjuncts of our great commercial transactions by which people are fed, warmed, clothed, and supplied with the implements and raw material of labor. There is, then, no reason why the railroads, which are only larger instruments of the same kind, should be omitted in the list of things that the government may manage and monopolize. It is surely of as much moment that a train-load of flour or butter should be carried with cheapness, certainty, **and** celerity from Chicago **to New** York, **as** that the despatch announcing its shipment or arrival **should be sent** in the same way ; and **if** we cannot **manage the latter to our satisfaction,** how shall we expect to manage **the former? As it will never do to have a** competitor in this carrying trade, the **government** must also take possession of all the canals. Of course these recommendations will, if adopted, largely increase **the** salaried officers **of** the country, and make our political contests tenfold **more** corrupt, acrimonious, and dangerous than now ; but as the Pennsylvania editor said **about** protection—" If protection is a good thing, we cannot have too **much** of it ! "—so say **we** of officials, the more the better.

But **we** see still larger fields that the government may occupy, this interference theory being established as the rule of its relation to the peo-**ple. As** the growing of wheat and the production of meats, to supply

* From the Chicago Evening Post.

the prime necessity of our nature for food, are of far more importance than the correspondence which occurs in getting the wheat and beef to the consumer or than the method of their transit; as the people must die if they have nothing to eat; as farming, as now done, is a careless, haphazard business, pursued without the aid of adequate machinery or the proper division of labor; as the cost of farm produce might, by the universal adoption of improved methods, be greatly cheapened, thus promoting the increase of the race, and adding immensely to the general happiness, the government ought, first of all, to take the agriculture of the country into its keeping. Then how easy, if it should be imposed upon by the men who make agricultural implements, to turn manufacturer at some hundred convenient places and make all the tools it might need. Just think of the immense advantage of being able to go to a government warehouse and get a barrel of flour for half what it now costs, or of stepping into government shambles from which, of course, the people will be fed, and getting a rib-roast or tenderloin steak at a figure that would make our city butchers ashamed. Of course, every farmer would be a government officer, sure of his pay, and without the most powerful stimulus to exertion; but if each man who handles a letter or sends or delivers a despatch is to have the livery of public service on his back, why not? Finally, as food is useless unless cooked, we see the necessity — still reasoning on premises which the telegraph men furnish — of having the cooking and management of the kitchens of the country turned over to such officers as the government shall select. For doing this, just as soon as the plan of governmental telegraphing is put into operation, the reasons will be entirely conclusive. What, we ask, can be of more importance than that our food should be of good quality, healthfully prepared, quickly and neatly served, and peacefully eaten. Put the National Telegraph by the side of the National Dinner, and see how it is dwarfed by the comparison. Contrast the annoyance of a telegram overcharged, missent, or delayed, with the unutterable horrors of indigestion. Look at our hotels, restaurants, and private houses, and see how cruelly the people suffer; then think how perfect, how quick, and how cheap the relief that the government might extend. We well know that, had government cooking always been the rule of the nation, the great rebellion would not have occurred. The war was the result of the bad food and worse kitchens of our brethren of the South. It had its origin in hot bread and hog, which ruined the stomachs, perverted the morals, and inflamed the worst passions of the South. As we have already sacrificed half a million of lives, and ten thousand millions of treasure to repair the consequences of government carelessness in suffering national cookshops to remain unestablished, we cannot make too much haste in opening them now.

But we have adduced examples enough to show the absurd conclusions to which the reasoning of these telegraphic schemers logically leads. Our government, good as it is, has objectionable features enough now. The disparities in the condition of the people are due more to the operation of unjust law than to differences in natural gifts; and the great source of mischief is in the usurpation by government of functions it ought never to exercise. We do most assuredly need reform; but we shall not find it in enlarging the sphere within which the government may act, nor in curtailing or circumscribing the liberty of the individual. Let us go in the other direction; and instead of making the paternal rule of Continental monarchies the object of imitation, let us extend the application of the American idea. Instead of clothing government with new powers, let us take from what it has. Instead of creating an army of new officers, let us dismiss half we have got. Instead of increasing the patronage of the executive and the causes of political contention, let us give greater simplicity to our system and greater security to the citizen and the state. Instead of training the people more and more to rely upon the government to supply their business, social, and educational wants, let us give greater scope to their individuality, so that they may more and more rely upon themselves. Our government differs from all other governments in the world in nothing so much as in its capacity of letting the people alone in their houses, their business, their religion, and their pleasure. Our people differ from all other peoples in nothing so much as in the fact that, comparatively, they are let alone. All that the country is, it owes to the partial freedom of its citizens to go where they please, do what they please, and think and speak their own thoughts; which freedom, by cultivating strength, self-reliance, enterprise, intelligence, and patriotism, has wrought the work we see before us. This freedom is to be still more extended over ground which inherited abuses now occupy, and the consequences will astonish the world!

No, no! Our government is not a wet-nurse for all the schemes which the ingenuity of men may invent, or which incomplete and half-seen considerations of public convenience may recommend. It is primarily an organization for the protection of person and property, and the punishment of crime. And to keep it within its sphere, and to disassociate it, as far as possible, from the usual business of the citizen, is to insure its life. Leave to the people all that individual or corporate effort may do, and they will do it well. Leave to the government the preservation of order and the punishment of crime, and the governed will have no reason to complain.

TELEGRAPHING BY GOVERNMENT.*

WE use the telegraph very extensively and pay it a good deal of money; so that there are few whose personal advantage from cheapening its use would be greater than our own; yet we do not regard with favor any of the bills looking to the establishment of a Government Telegraph. Here are some of our reasons: —

I. The prevalent tendency in our day is toward a further restriction rather than an enlargement of the sphere of government. We have (for instance) a good many public markets in this city, which are, for the most part, public nuisances. Had the city left this whole business of purveying free to private enterprise, only overseeing it in the interest of public health, few can doubt that our supply of food would have been better and cheaper than it is. The same is the case with many other at-

* From the New York Tribune.

tempts to serve or save the citizen through the agency of government. Most certainly, we would not limit the sphere of government to the mere prevention of breaking heads and picking pockets; but we should ponder long before enlarging it.

II. A Government Telegraph is usually proposed as an adjunct of the post-office. Our government already claims and enforces a monopoly of the business of carrying letters, charges its own prices, collects some $15,000,000 a year from the people for letter-carrying, and then loses some $6,000,000 a year by the business. We submit that it should show a better balance-sheet on this account before extending its sphere of operations.

III. We never owned any telegraph stock, and expect to own none; we are a daily and heavy customer to telegraphs, and expect to live and die such. We presume that a Government Telegraph would somewhat cheapen the cost of messages; but the money invested in establishing it would never be returned to the treasury. The clamor for a reduction of charges (as now with letters) would steadily overbear any hope of profit. Can it be right, we ask, to tax the whole people for the benefit of that small minority who send messages by telegraph? Would it not be better to start government establishments for potato-growing on a gigantic scale, so as to supply the poor cheaply with wholesome and nourishing food? Where one wants cheap messages, many would be benefited by having a sure and ample supply of cheap potatoes.

IV. Government, in this and other free countries, is and must be largely an affair of party. The government of this country has been, is, and must be, to a great extent, the rule of the dominant party. Would it be well to have the telegraph under the absolute control of either party in an excited Presidential election? Could the outs safely use it? Could the people implicitly trust it? Remember how the mails were rifled under Jackson, with the tacit approval of Postmaster-General Kendall, on the assumption that it was right to take and burn Abolition documents if circulated in Slave States. Consider General Jackson's and Governor Marcy's official recommendations that the circulation of such documents be prohibited by law. We should not like to have the telegraph controlled, throughout the ensuing Presidential canvasses, by our political adversaries, nor yet by our political friends.

V. The government is heavily in debt, and its finances are not in good condition; yet it is bored and importuned for subsidies on this side and on that, — all of them on the pretence of public advantage, many of them with just grounds for such assumption. If the Northern and Southern Pacific Railroads could both be built within the next five years, we believe they would add five hundred millions of dollars to our national wealth within the twenty years succeeding. We demur to their present construction by government aid, simply that the state of our finances forbids it. But if our government is able to build telegraphs where they are not wanted, why not railroads where they are the very first necessity of settlement and civilization?

We might go on for an hour longer, but let the above suffice for the present. We think the government should let the telegraph business alone.

www.ingramcontent.com/pod-product-compliance
Lightning Source LLC
Chambersburg PA
CBHW030610270326
41927CB00007B/1112